REPGOLD

A Step-by-Step Guide to
Successfully Repair and Build Your Online Reputation

REPGOLD

A Step-by-Step Guide to
Successfully Repair and Build Your Online Reputation

EDWARD M. YANG

Cover design by Ivica Jandrijevic
Interior layout and design by www.writingnights.org
Book preparation by Chad Robertson
Edited by Robert Astle, Highline Editorial, New York, NY
Indexing and Proofreading: Marianne Steiger

ISBN: 978-1-7339131-0-2

Disclaimer A: Any legal advice herein is offered solely as the opinion and research of the author, and it is strongly advised that any legal questions be directed to a bona fide attorney.

Disclaimer B: As with any book that deals with technology, it will always run the risk of making references to companies or technologies that have already ended up in the dustbins of history. Once-dominant brands of today can quickly be the forgotten brands of tomorrow. The author has kept the information as contemporary and up-to-date as possible up until the date of publication. However, the author recognizes that current internet giants could completely vanish from the online environment.

Biblical References: New International Version
Printed in the United States of America.
Printed on acid-free paper.

24 23 22 21 20 19 18 17 8 7 6 5 4 3 2 1

To my late father, Dr. Jack Yang. He taught me through his life that a person's reputation is built through loving action.

To my mother, Theresa Yang, who has always showed me unconditional love through her years of sacrifice.

Dear children, let us not love with words or speech but with actions and in truth.

—1 John 3:18

TABLE OF CONTENTS

FOREWORD

I met Edward during our undergraduate days at UBC in Vancouver, British Columbia. Even back then he was always a straight shooter, and unafraid to tell things as they were with refreshing honesty. From there, he moved to California and started an award-winning PR agency that helped advise brands on how to build their reputation. When I went solo and started my own agency career, Edward gave me inspiration and hope. He told me two things: never give up and treat your customer's reputation like gold.

I've taken those words to heart every single day. Edward is my beacon for life and business advice, and his new book "RepGold" is a true must-read for those whose businesses are impacted by their online reputation…which is all of us.

Dean Ara
Principal at Total Product Marketing
www.totalproductmarketing.com

INTRODUCTION

My late father did his best to impart to me certain nuggets of wisdom that he thought would serve me well through my life. Some of them, like "drink lots of water to cure what ails you," seemed a bit quirky but harmless. But one that stuck with me my whole life and has helped me create a business that assists other businesses is that *a person's reputation is worth more than gold.*

Money can come and go. But your reputation, once out there, is very difficult to change. It's hard to repair a damaged reputation, but it's so easy to damage a good reputation.

Think of a clear glass of purified water that is perfect for drinking. Then imagine taking an eyedropper and squeezing in a few drops of black ink. That clear water becomes stained pretty quickly.

Reputation is similar. A business can be torn down with insane speed because of the viral nature of the algorithms embedded in the internet, which is then accelerated by real-time social media and trolls and then spread faster than the speed of sound.

In the past there was obviously no need for online reputation management since most people weren't browsing, buying, or selling online. Reputation was what you built through mass media advertising and promoted through public relations in newspapers or on television or radio. This was an expensive undertaking, and generally only large corporations or famous personalities could afford to hire publicists to control and disseminate their messages.

Small businesses built their reputations primarily through word of mouth, and the extent of building a brand or destroying it was limited to how fast or far the word of mouth could go.

Today, it's a whole new (and bewildering) ballgame. What this book imparts to the reader is my deep understanding of how to establish and maintain online reputations. Like any good coach, I provide a step-by step guide for all kinds of consumers, small-business owners, large corporations, and marketers to first understand the issues. Then I provide practical answers *and* tools that are both information-rich and easy to read.

Small businesses can be hurt immensely by negative reviews on Google My Business, Yelp, TripAdvisor, Amazon, and specialized consumer complaint websites like Pissed Consumer or Ripoff Report. To make matters worse, 280 characters on Twitter or a post on Facebook can go viral, then global, in a matter of seconds.

This is magnified for large companies, brands, and people. Bad press can lead to a rapidly spreading narrative that even the most seasoned corporate communications team would be hard-pressed to get ahead of.

We see this in the news on a daily basis:

- Toyota's brake issues, which led to cars allegedly being unable to stop, according to crash victims who drove Toyotas.
- Chipotle suffered through a rash of food-poisoning cases that led to a decline in store visitors and a related decline in its stock price.
- US airlines were captured on smartphone video allegedly mistreating passengers, the most prominent case being that

of Dr. David Dao, who was dragged off a United Airlines flight.
- Even well-known personalities are not immune. Former secretary of state and presidential candidate Hillary Clinton saw suppressed favorability ratings due to the drawn-out controversy regarding her private email server.

For these reasons, it is imperative that any business—whether it is a single dentist or a large Fortune 500 corporation—be both vigilant and proactive when it comes to protecting its online reputation.

Yet for all the diligence, there are bound to be times when an irritated customer or even a disgruntled employee or ex-employee will go on the internet and vent. Google may display part of that tirade through a multitude of ways—star ratings on review sites, directly on a Google My Business listing, or on a complaint site like Ripoff Report.

It is that moment when the first page of search results displays a complaint that work must be done to try to blunt its impact. Let's be very clear here: I am not advocating that you "game" the system by "tricking" Google. Even if that were to work in the short run, with the rapid pace that Google iterates its search algorithm, there are no guarantees it would continue to work in the long run.

To achieve what I call "Total Online Reputation," my approach is a much deeper and preventive approach. I will help you establish a daily routine so that you can maintain a strong online presence, and I provide the precise tools to give you every advantage to build and maintain that presence. If you are already dealing with negative feedback about your product or service, you are starting from behind. But my book addresses all the issues you are confronting and how to correct *most* of them.

That's what I aim to provide you here: a blueprint that any company can use to fight back against seemingly impossible odds. Whether you're a business owner, a public relations manager, an

SEO specialist, a marketing manager, or anyone in between, my specific recommendations will add many tools to your toolkit to use for many years to come. So before running to the phone and calling a publicist or expert in online reputation repair, I suggest you read this guide carefully, as there are many ways to skin a cat, and many ways to solve your online issues.

This book will provide you with all the tools you'll need, no matter what your experience level is with marketing. Whether you're completely new or have years of experience, many tips in this book can help you no matter your comfort level.

Edward M. Yang
Managing Partner, Firecracker PR
Founder, RepGold

1

THE IMPORTANCE OF ONLINE REPUTATION

THE GROWING THREAT

It's hard to imagine a time when our lives didn't center around the internet. The stunning speed at which a generation has shifted its focus of activity for their social and professional lives from offline to online has been breathtaking to witness, even for those in the middle of it.

Traditional forms of media have been disintermediated while new forms of disseminating information have dominated. Information that used to only be held in the archives of libraries or in the minds of experts is now easily within reach via a smartphone. Through search engines like Google, literally any information can be found in a matter of seconds. The online community-sourced encyclopedia Wikipedia has rendered the Encyclopedia Britannica a quaint collector's item rather than a staple for every household.

Because of this, consumers can learn more about a product or service than ever before possible as they make their purchasing decisions. Research consistently shows that over 90 percent of consumers research online before making a purchasing decision. This isn't limited to the B2C (business to consumer) space only: a 2014 State of B2B Procurement study by Acquity Group[1] found that 94 percent of business buyers do some form of online research. The same study showed that 77 percent used Google.

Beyond just buying things, online reputation has a growing impact on job seekers. A 2016 study by CareerBuilder and Harris Poll showed about 60 percent of employers use social media networks to research job candidates, up from 52 percent the year before.[2] You can be sure that number will continue to climb as baby boomers retire and are replaced by a tech-savvy younger generation whose first move will be to Google a person's name before they're anywhere close to a job interview.

If the quote by Milan Kundera is correct—"business has only two functions—marketing and innovation"[3]—then anything that has such a potentially huge impact on your brand perception must take priority.

"The best place to hide a dead body is page 2 of Google's search results."

Research by Hubspot in 2014 found that 75 percent of users never scroll past the first page of search results.[4] That means that those six-plus listings that come up on the first page of Google will

---

[1] https://www.accenture.com/t20150624T211502__w__/us-
   en/_acnmedia/Accenture/Conversion-
   Assets/DotCom/Documents/Global/PDF/Industries_15/Accenture-B2B-Procurement-
   Study.pdf

[2] https://www.prnewswire.com/news-releases/number-of-employers-using-social-media-to-
   screen-candidates-has-increased-500-percent-over-the-last-decade-300258537.html

[3] https://www.economist.com/blogs/schumpeter/2012/09/z-business-quotations

[4] https://blog.hubspot.com/insiders/inbound-marketing-stats

be pretty much all someone will see before they click further to learn more.

According to the BrightLocal Local Consumer Review Survey 2018:[5]

- 86% of consumers read reviews for local businesses (including 95% of people aged 18-34)
- Consumers read an average of 10 online reviews before feeling able to trust a local business
- 40% of consumers only take into account reviews written within the past 2 weeks – up from 18% last year
- 57% of consumers will only use a business if it has 4 or more stars
- 80% of 18-34-year olds have written online reviews – compared to just 41% of consumers over 55
- 91% of 18-34-year-old consumers trust online reviews as much as personal recommendations
- 89% of consumers read businesses' responses to reviews

It should be noted that although there are many search engines, when we refer to online reputation in this book, we will be mainly referring to Google. This is simply because of the sheer dominance of Google's search, to the point where their company name has become a verb ("go Google that information yourself") and a synonym for search engines.

At the pace that technology changes, this by no way means that Google will always be number one. The strategies and tactics we teach to achieve Total Online Reputation will benefit you no matter what search engine we're talking about. When you pay attention to the basics, a lot of good things will happen from a reputation standpoint.

The emergence of the internet has empowered consumers in ways that could never be foreseen. Now it is easy to quickly whip out a

---

[5] https://www.brightlocal.com/learn/local-consumer-review-survey/

smartphone and Google a restaurant name to see how many stars and reviews are on its Yelp page, then decide whether or not to give them your business. Prior to this, prospective customers had to rely on the professional critic (whether it be movie, restaurant, or newspaper writer) or on word of mouth.

This empowering of the consumer is a double-edged sword for companies. On the one hand, it has created an incentive to make sure they provide the best service possible and to resolve conflicts when they occur, lest they end up on the internet forever. On the other hand, it has created a Wild Wild West environment where anyone can post anything they want without regard for accuracy and truth. After all, who is the arbiter between a "he said, she said" conflict?

What does this mean for large companies or small businesses who don't know what or even how to evaluate the state of their online reputation? They are running a huge risk that their brand could be suffering from continuous damage without even knowing about it. Worse, the relative permanence of content indexed on search engines means that a customer who received a widget that was broken and then had to spend hours communicating with customer service to convince them it had arrived that way … his angst can be poured out and codified forever on the internet for everyone to see.

THE BEST DEFENSE IS A GOOD OFFENSE

Below is a sample narrative of a typical start-up that unfortunately has to deal with a series of damaging online reputation issues.

Maria and Peter opened a little shop using their famous cupcake recipe that Maria was given by her family. Their new labor of love, Dreamy Cupcakes, had finally come true! Both had quit their day jobs to take a shot and pursue the American dream. Much of the encouragement to open Dreamy Cupcakes was from family and friends who insisted that such delicious cupcakes shouldn't be kept a secret. With the support of loved ones, Maria and Peter took the leap into the unknown.

Dreamy Cupcakes, as a new business, is starting with a clean slate. So far there have been no customers and no reviews (good or bad). Why would they even need online reputation at this stage?

In many forms of competition—football, chess, even war—there is a saying that the best defense is a good offense. In essence, this means that by being proactive and taking the fight to your opponent, you reduce the vulnerability of sitting back on defense and being reactive.

In regard to online reputation, your "opponent" isn't a clearly defined singular entity. Rather, it is the opponent of unhappy customers or lying agitators that seek to strike down your reputation online. Using the analogy of warfare, this is similar to the difference between fighting a war against a clearly defined enemy flying a nation's flag on their vehicles versus fighting a war against a terrorist insurgency group that blends into the crowd.

For any company that places an importance on how their brand is perceived, a good offense is crucial. There may be very few unique situations where this doesn't apply, for instance in an industry that has only one monopolistic competitor. In all other situations where there is a relatively free market, any damage to your online reputation may drive business to your competitors.

You may not feel the impact of negative online reputation immediately, but just like the frog sitting serenely in a pot of water slowly increasing in temperature, the ultimate consequence could be devastating when it is too late. "Death by a thousand cuts" is another way to look at it. One bad review on its own may not matter. But add up bad reviews or complaints on Yelp, Ripoff Report, Pissed Consumer, and media news articles, and the damage could be irrevocable.

As an example, a client of ours owned a chain of brake-repair shops that suffered some online complaints. By reading the complaints, you could clearly see a common theme of what was bugging the customers. Their sales were stagnant. It's actually not hard to figure out why. Bad experiences spread quickly online and by word of mouth. Anyone who had a subpar experience would not only avoid returning, they'd also likely influence family, friends, and strangers to avoid the brake shops. This type of vicious cycle of negative reviews can actually mean the difference between a thriving business and one that's headed for ruin.

This book will give you practical steps to repair your online reputation as best you can if there are already negative reviews out there. If there aren't, keeping in mind the adage of a good offense, we will give you steps to "immunize" your online brand and position yourself in the best possible manner to fend off the inevitable future attacks. Because no matter how good you perceive your service to be, it's only a matter of time before one of your customers becomes unhappy for any number of reasons.

This book will give you practical steps to:

- Understand the importance of online reputation management.
- Repair your online reputation in the event it is damaged, using both quick short-term fixes and long-term solutions.
- Immunize your online reputation if it is currently considered clean and unsullied, positioning yourself in the best possible manner to fend off inevitable future attacks.
- Monitor your online reputation so you can respond quickly and put out any sparks before they become fires.

As with any guide, all the solutions I propose may or may not be effective depending on your exact situation and how much damage has been done to your reputation. A positive outcome may require the help of a professional public relations agency. But at the very least, this book will arm you with sufficient knowledge to tackle many situations yourself.

WHY YOU NEED ONLINE REPUTATION MANAGEMENT (ORM)

Dreamy Cupcakes has been on a roll. Its first store opened to wide acclaim, and word of mouth quickly spread on social media about their delicious, moist cupcakes. Their business won numerous foodie awards, and they give back to their community so that they became known as a socially conscious brand. Maria and Peter's growing business continues to receive positive feedback on review sites, and they've also issued a few press releases on new products.

One day Peter was Googling their business name and came across a negative review of their cupcakes. Puzzled because he'd never heard of a complaint, he clicked on it to read further. The headline read "Dreamy Cupcakes a Nightmare … Service SUCKS!!!" It was posted by a local food blogger. Apparently she had come in a couple weeks prior and received the wrong cupcakes, then to make matters worse, received what she claimed was really poor service from the employee.

Peter's heart sank. He knew exactly who the employee was. Peter had fired the guy a week ago for not behaving responsibly, but apparently it was too late to prevent him from inflicting damage on their store.

Out of the corner of his eye, he saw the Yelp listing for his store. He clicked on it, and with a sinking feeling, he saw a one-star review. It looked like it was left by the same blogger. She was mad enough about what happened that she was posting her bad experience far and wide.

Dreamy Cupcakes' experience isn't unusual. It happens to individuals, small businesses, and large enterprises every day.

There are *three* main reasons why any individual, professional, or company might need online reputation management.

The first is to project a positive image of yourself. You might believe your company has a great story and cares deeply about its customers. And perhaps it does. But unless there's an easy way for people to find that information, it will simply be buried and lost in the billions of web pages out there. ORM can help promote your mission and communicate your story in a way that is easy to find.

If you can help your client or yourself constantly maintain a good image and get good reviews and positive feedback, Google remembers this. That is to say that Google is a very, very "smart" search engine. It looks at all the data out there about your client or your company. It virtually summarizes the data, then decides whether a certain article is worthy of being displayed on page 1 or not.

If this sounds like public relations and corporate communications to you, you're on the right track. Both PR and corporate communications are there to get the information and stories out to position a company in a positive manner. ORM is an extension of this but focused primarily on search engines and social media (thus the *O* for "online"). You're not concerned about things like TV interviews, radio interviews, billboard ads, and the like *unless* they have an online component.

For instance, a TV interview for your client is great but won't concern your ORM work. That is unless the TV station carries a video clip of the interview on their website, or it's posted on YouTube or some other online video site. Then it impacts what you're doing greatly. A radio interview itself also won't impact your ORM work, unless the radio station carries it in the form of a podcast, or has a web page dedicated to that interview, or has the transcript of that interview in text form on a web page. Then, because there's an online component, it greatly impacts what you're doing as well.

Here are some types of positive things you may want to promote in the hopes that they reach the first page of Google:

- Strong sales growth
- New prominent executive hired
- Awards they've won
- Community work and charitable donations
- Happy customers

Again, note that these are exactly the types of stories that PR would want to work on. And that is why PR plays a big part in our Total Online Reputation formula. Don't worry if you have zero experience in PR. Later in this book we'll give you some valuable hands-on information in the chapter "Public Relations" that you can use to get PR off the ground.

The second is to suppress or dilute negative information. Most companies come across ORM when they are desperate and looking to combat negative information about them, usually in the form of complaints. ORM can help to push down these negative search results by promoting the positive search results.

It goes without saying that, whether it's on their smartphones or home or work computers, people will hit search engines first and type in a company's name, or the name of a product or service, or the name of a doctor, dentist, accountant, or lawyer or any other type of professional.

You'll notice that most reputation-repair companies advertise that they will remove negative results, but if you delve into their small print, they don't really promise that. Instead, they say they will try to push negative results down off of the first page of Google. That's quite different from permanently removing negative results.

In Total Online Reputation, we'll teach you some tried-and-true tactics that we've personally used to great success in permanently *removing* negative results … not just pushing them down. This isn't always possible, but it definitely is doable—we've done it. And believe me, if you can succeed in getting a negative result removed permanently, your client is going to love you and sing your praises day and night.

One of our earliest clients was a timeshare company whose first page of Google was tattooed with negative results and complaints. Using an early version of the formula we teach, I managed to whittle it down to *just one* negative result on the first page—a huge difference.

Another client sold security cameras and had *just three* negative listings out of ten on the first page. Again, using the same techniques we teach you right here, we got rid of all three of them … *permanently*.

In the event that the negative results can't be permanently removed, then yes, you'll have to work by pushing them off the first page of search engines. The way this is done is through leapfrogging. What I mean is that you want to get other positive search results to rank higher than the bad one. If you get enough of them ranked higher, the bad one falls off of the first page naturally.

You'll also notice I keep saying "first page." Why not more than that? Well, research shows that 90 percent of searchers don't go past the first page of search engine results, so if you can get it off the first page, that's a huge first step in making sure that 90 percent of searchers (or more) won't ever see the bad result.

Therefore, when it comes to suppressing negative results, that should be your number-one objective: get multiple search results to dominate the first page of Google so that the one bad one falls to page two.

The third is to assist people in finding you. Most people start their search using a search engine—more often than not, Google. They directly type in the name of the person, company, or product to get more information. If your name or your company's name is common, you want to make it so that you rise above the rest when someone types in your name in a search engine. ORM can help rank your results as high up on a page as possible where a searcher has the greatest chance of finding you.

This is sometimes the case when your name is shared by other companies in different cities, states, or countries. If it's a professional like a doctor or lawyer, their name might also be shared by other professionals.

In fact, people will still type a company's name into Google even when they know the URL! It could be because they're too lazy to try to guess the actual URL, or it could just be force of habit. Whatever the reason, you want to make sure that you come up as high as possible for these "branded" search terms.

If you follow the above steps correctly, online reputation management will help you solve most of the issues in all three areas.

Waiting Until It's Too Late

Since old adages always have ways of applying to our world today, when it comes to online reputation, an ounce of prevention truly is worth a pound of cure.

Big online reputation agencies charge thousands if not tens of thousands of dollars per month to help brands with negative listings on search engines. The strategies and tactics you'll learn in this book will give you the knowledge to outdo even them.

The truth of the matter is that most of these big ORM agencies make a living on "churning and burning." That is, their business model cares less about happy customers and more about signing up new customers. Ironically, these ORM agencies have generated plenty of negative online reviews. The only real way to separate the effective ORM agencies from the scammers is to get testimonials from companies they successfully helped.

Total Online Reputation is about creating a *comprehensive* plan around repairing and immunizing your online brand that is far more powerful than what these ORM agencies can do. *It is about being authentic, honest, and caring.*

The time to get started is now. Procrastination is your biggest enemy. Sitting and saying "I'll address this tomorrow" simply means that tomorrow will never arrive. By the time you run into negative reviews, tomorrow could be too late.

The best way to defeat procrastination is through small steps. In his book *Mini Habits: Small Habits, Bigger Results* (CreateSpace Independent Publishing Platform, 2013), Stephen Guise shows how to get moving by just doing one simple action. The example he uses is doing one push-up. The thought of going through a thirty-minute workout is enough to make most of us sit back down and reach for the Doritos. But all of us could get up and do one push-up. And that one push-up inevitably leads to many more. But the key is getting started on that first pushup, or that first action that breaks the cycle of procrastination.

S. J. Scott, author of *Habit Stacking: 97 Small Life Changes That Take Five Minutes or Less* (Oldtown Publishing LLC, 2014), puts it another way. "The core idea behind the mini-habits concept is that you can build a major habit by thinking small enough to get started. Most people don't need motivation to do one push-up, so it's easy to get started. And once you get going, you'll find it's easy to keep at it."

Your goal is to get moving on some mini-habits around any of the steps we teach you. Pick the one that seems the easiest and do that first. It doesn't have to take more than ten or fifteen minutes.

At the risk of wearing out the adages, I'll add one more: "a journey of a thousand miles begins with the first step."

Let's get started.

2

THE TOTAL ONLINE
REPUTATION PROGRAM

GOALS AND STRATEGY

The goals of my Total Online Reputation program are:

- To take a **proactive** approach in *promoting positive information* about a person's name, company reputation, or product brand
- To aggressively **combat** *negative comments* or search results as they come up
- To **protect** an existing brand or person's reputation to the fullest extent possible
- To **respond** to negative information as close to real time as

      possible
- To ultimately **delight** your customers and prospects

Total Online Reputation is a plan I've created that merges the marketing disciplines of search engine optimization (SEO), public relations (PR), social media marketing, and good old- fashioned customer service. It may also involve other tasks such as website design and online research.

But before you get overwhelmed and decide you can't do this because you have no experience in these areas, we've set up each chapter with easy-to-follow instructions on how to do them. It doesn't matter if you have an MBA or didn't graduate high school. Just follow our clear guidelines on each task and you'll start to see results.

Total Online Reputation is primarily about three core strategies:

- Repairing
- Immunizing
- Monitoring

Some will need repairing in a desperate way immediately. Others won't but will want to immunize their name against future attacks. All should require monitoring.

I will get into each of these in greater detail later in the book.

THE TOTAL ONLINE REPUTATION FORMULA

Without further ado, here is the Total Online Reputation formula that will help you absolutely dominate online reputation management. This formula is something that most large reputation firms are not doing. At most, they're likely doing one or two parts of it, and even then not very well. The power of the formula is how each part strengthens and reinforces the other. Thus, when the entire formula is firing on all cylinders, it creates a competitive advantage that is tough to overcome.

The total online formula for dominating online reputation management is:

$$ORM = SEO + PR + SM + CS^2$$

This stands for:

Online Reputation Management = Search Engine Optimization + Public Relations + Social Media + Customer Service and Common Sense

Rather than thinking of the formula as a "secret sauce," it is a step-by-step process that really works when the combination of the formula components is matched with hard work, delivering the results for your business, no matter how large or small you are.

Mastering this simple formula will have your customers raving about you and ensure that positive word of mouth will have prospects willing to pay a premium for your products or services.

How much time should you spend on each of these areas? Well, like anything in life, it depends. You'll have to do a diagnosis of your current clients and see how they score.

That will dictate how much time you'll need on SEO, PR, and social media, all underpinned with you providing great customer service based on good common sense.

Now let's take a closer look at this formula:

SEO—Search Engine Optimization

For those of you who are in marketing, you will know what SEO means and are likely familiar with how it works, along with basic best practices.

For those who aren't familiar with the term SEO, it simply means doing things to make your website more relevant and thus rank higher in Google. It's the most technical aspect of the ORM secret formula to success. But don't worry if you're not technical at all as we break down everything into easily understandable bite-size morsels.

SEO is the primary, and sometimes only, weapon that most online reputation management companies out there have. Remember that our secret formula will be teaching you much more.

So Why Is SEO That Important?

Well, remember that the ultimate goal of ORM is to have positive mentions of your or your client's company name, product brand name, or personal name on the first page of search engines while keeping it free from negative mentions.

To that end, SEO is going to be critical.

It means making websites that have content and information that is useful to the visitor, which Google will like and bless with a higher ranking. It means finding sites that already have high authority that you can help move higher in the rankings, essentially piggybacking on them to get onto Google's page 1.

It means doing link building when necessary to bump these sites up. Link building is almost half of the importance of SEO, so good-quality links to the sites that you either create or get listed on will be very important.

It means understanding what makes for a good website that search engines love, like the website's layout, its structure, the quality and usefulness of its content, having the right tags, and again the links that point to the site.

If you do not have any background with SEO, do not worry. It's actually not as difficult as it seems. It just requires a certain mindset. If you know how Google acts and what types of websites people like, you can easily be successful in SEO. I'll show you how.

Personally, I had no training in SEO. At the time, SEO was so new that there really was no formal training out there. It was through trial and error, reading books, and blogs on the subject that I figured out what works and what doesn't. Even today, the field of SEO is changing so rapidly that the tactics that worked even a couple of years ago may not be effective at all today. But sticking with the strategies outlined in this book will position you for success no matter how Google changes their formula.

If you already are familiar with SEO, that's great. We may provide you with some tactics that you might not have thought of, especially in thinking about how other areas of SEO can be blended to achieve positive ORM results.

PR—Public Relations

Bill Gates is quoted as having said, "If I only had a dollar left, I would spend it on PR."

Public relations is about getting positive media coverage.

There are all sorts of tools within the realm of PR to help get press coverage, including press releases, product/service reviews, interviews, thought-leadership articles, guest posts, surveys, and events. Let's go over some of the most important ones here:

Press releases: A press release is a formal announcement written for the purpose of making some news "official." Note that "PR" doesn't stand for press release, it stands for *public relations.* A release is just a tool and it is not the entirety of PR. Businesses generally write press releases when they have something important to announce such as a new product launch, an event, an important hire, a promotion, or anything considered newsworthy.

Product/service reviews: Most people who are considering buying a new product or signing up for a new service will search online for reviews. This makes sense; why would you commit to something without first quickly checking to see what others have to say about it? You can pitch your product or service to the press or influencers early and try to get them to write a positive review.

Interviews: A well-conducted interview can be a fantastic way to add depth and context to your message. Interviews can be on TV, radio, newspaper, websites, podcasts, or even streamed on Facebook Live. Putting a face behind a company's name can be an effective way to personalize your brand.

Thought-leadership articles: Also known as guest opinion articles, guest posts, editorials, opinion pieces, and more. These are usually written in a non-promotional tone, and they are meant to educate the reader while staking out your credibility as a leader in this space.

Surveys: Who doesn't love reading the results of surveys? The press certainly loves it. That's why you will often find news stories about the latest survey results on this or that. Why not commission a survey yourself and get some press out of it?

Events: Live events are a tried-and-true way to get coverage. But these days as news rooms are faced with budgetary cuts, it's harder to get the press to show up to an event. Consider attending industry trade shows or carrying out promotional events that will draw a lot of people.

A well-thought-out and sustained PR strategy can pay dividends beyond just on the ORM side. It could have a huge impact on your overall sales.

That's because the return on investment (ROI) of PR is superior to almost every other form of marketing if you do it right. And that's the key: doing PR right.

Why is PR so powerful in the quest for online reputation management? The answer is simple: because search engines love websites with "authority." This means websites such as Wikipedia but also the *New York Times*, CNET, Fox News, etc. Basically any major website that people already go to for news and information.

So logically it makes sense that if your brand is mentioned in a story on a news website, it should come up quite high on search engine results when people search for your brand or company name.

In Total Online Reputation, we'll give you all the basics as well as secret advanced strategies that even many PR pros either don't know or don't use. You will find much of the information is common sense mixed in with some of the simple tactics that I've laid out.

NB: Some of you may have little or no experience with PR and may think, "I really can't do this. It's too hard." I'm positive that after reading my book, you will definitely have all the tools to start developing a coherent PR plan that supports and protects your online reputation.

SM—Social Media

These days every company knows they need social media and that they have to get around to doing it, but few are actually doing it effectively. They create a Facebook or Twitter site, post once a week, and call it a day. And then whenever anybody asks about your social media strategy, you tell them you have one and that it's not what you expected or that maybe social media isn't for you.

That's not really social media.

Google and other search engines love social media, which makes sense. Social media sites have everything Google loves: relevant content, fresh content, rapid refreshing of content, user engagement, and authority. For that very reason, social media is a big part of managing online reputation management.

The best part is, most of you will likely be familiar with using social media just from your daily personal or professional lives, so it won't seem very foreign or difficult to you.

CS²—Customer Service and Common Sense

The last part of my formula is CS squared, which stands for Customer Service and Common Sense.

The key to protecting a brand against complaints in the first place is exceptional customer service and, secondly, having a commonsense plan to directly deal with customer complaints.

These days, everyone pays lip service to superior customer service. A few companies do it really well and it should be no surprise that they reap massive benefits including loyal customers, positive viral word of mouth, repeat purchases, and strong revenue growth.

The good news is that customer service is something that can be trained and ingrained into a company's culture. Once it is, it creates a formidable competitive advantage.

In a 2011 article in *Psychology Today*,[6] the writer *Dr. Jim Taylor* defines common sense as "sound judgment derived from experience rather than study." There's also debate about whether common sense is something you are born with or something you can learn and improve on.

As it relates to customer service, some typical mistakes that companies make can be identified and rectified. Our "Customer Service" section in this book will work to make you a star in the eyes of your customers.

So in closing, let's sum it up again:

$$ORM = SEO + PR + SM + CS^2$$

That is the Total Online Reputation formula. And that, if done with persistence, will help repair your bad reputation, immunize you from future complaints, and ensure your company has a solid foundation for years to come. But even if, after reading this book, you understand the basics and still feel you need expert help, there are a myriad of online reputation experts who can help you plan and execute the right strategy for you.

---

[6] https://www.psychologytoday.com/us/blog/the-power-prime/201107/common-sense-is-neither-common-nor-sense

ASSESSING THE PROBLEM

The first step in solving any problem is conducting an assessment. After all, how can you come up with a diagnosis if you don't understand what's wrong? A thorough and honest review of how severe the problem is will dictate the necessary actions needed. The specific strategies taught in this book are applied to different situations; it is not one size fits all. Here are the steps you can take to assess if a problem exists and how serious it may be.

1. Search Google.
   Google is by far the most dominant search engine on the planet. Therefore, any search for the purposes of online reputation management should focus on Google until (or if) the day comes that some other search engine supplants them in market share.
   Simply type in the name you are looking to fix or protect. This could be the name of a person. It could be the name of a company. It could be the name of a product or service. Whatever it is you are concerned about protecting, that's the name to do a search on.

2. Tally mentions.
   The average search engine results page (SERP) will have about six to ten search results. Scan the results and make a tally of how many are about you. Make sure to distinguish between similar-sounding companies or people that might not be you.

3. Classify as positive, negative, or neutral.
   For the ones that are about you, note if it is a positive listing, a negative listing, or a neutral one.
   An example of a positive listing would be aggregated review on a site such as Yelp or TripAdvisor that had more than 3.5

out of 5 stars. Or it could be a positive YouTube video review. It could be a press mention or press review that was good.

Examples of a negative listing would be anything that comes up from complaint sites such as Ripoff Report, Pissed Consumer, Complaints Board, or any other similar sites.

A negative listing could also be a story in the news that portrayed you in a bad light. It could be a blog post that was critical of you. It could be forum comments on message boards that are complaints as well.

Neutral listings are those that are fact-based such as local directories, stock ticker symbols, and the like.

4. Examine negative search results.

Take a closer look at the negative search results. What are they exactly? And how many complaints are there? If there are posted complaints on a site such as Ripoff Report, how many postings are there?

The reason this is important is because search engines such as Google factor in things like how many posts are on a site about a company. A Ripoff Report page with 150 bad reviews will be far harder to push down than a Ripoff Report page with only two bad reviews.

Similarly, a bad review in the *Los Angeles Times* will be far harder to push down than a bad review on a blog that no one has heard of.

4. Check Google's suggested searches.

You may have noticed that when you start typing a search term in Google, even while you are typing, you will see suggested search terms come up in a drop-down menu. Start typing your name, and see if any of the suggested search terms are negative.

For example, if your company were called Dreamy Cupcakes, you would start by typing "Dreamy Cupcakes" and see if any of the suggested terms pop up on your screen, such as "Dreamy Cupcakes scam," "Dreamy Cupcakes lies," or "Dreamy Cupcakes complaints." Those terms are generated by Google based on search volume. If enough people are searching about it, they will come up.

Also, on the very bottom of Google's search results page, you will see a section called "Searches related to XYZ …." Check to see if any of the related searches are negative as well. If there are negative suggested searches in either case, note what they're called.

Now you have a more complete picture of your online reputation health. This can simply be tracked in a spreadsheet, ideally Google Sheets, so you can share it with whomever you need to.

If the search results page shows mostly *positive and neutral* search results, congratulations! Your main priority should be in keeping it that way. Immunizing yourself and sticking to providing stellar customer service will be your main goals.

If your search results page is mostly *neutral*, your goal is to start getting your business some positive listings to create goodwill and a stronger reputation.

If your search results page has ***more negatives than positives***, your first priority is to do whatever you can to repair your reputation using the strategies outlined in this book.

ANALYZING THE COMPETITION

One of the best ways to get a jumpstart in online reputation is to see what your direct competitors are doing.

To begin, try typing their brand name into Google and seeing what search results come up. From those results, make a list of websites that they appear on, and note which your own should be on. For Dreamy Cupcakes, it could be:

- A dessert or sweets directory
- A listing of local food outlets
- A food magazine or blog that they should target as well, or a local newspaper food critic
- YouTube video reviews of the best cupcakes in the city

Paste the URL into a spreadsheet, and add whether it is neutral, negative, or positive. An easy way to organize the spreadsheet is to have a tab for each competitor.

Also categorize the websites you find into three groupings: owned, third party, and earned.

Owned websites are just that: websites where you own and control 100 percent of the content. These include the corporate or company home page. Within the site itself, it can include pages for blogs, contact information, and a range of pages that offer services or products for sale, for reservations, or for future orders. Owned websites have their URL purchased and the site built out by the company itself.

It is also important to note that *third-party* sites are split into two subcategories. There are websites where you can add content and control: social media profile pages such as Facebook, LinkedIn, Twitter, Pinterest, Instagram. There are websites you cannot control and *must* pay attention to such as **Yelp**, **TripAdvisor**, **Better Business Bureau**, and websites potentially hazardous to your business like **Pissed Consumer**.

Earned websites are those for which you need to do something unique or special to have your content or news appear on them. Typically this involves press coverage on a well-known news site or blog, for instance the *Los Angeles Times* or Huffington Post. You cannot buy your way onto a news site, thus the label "earned." Other terms you might be familiar with include "public relations" or "media relations."

I always insist when browsing for the first time for research that you go deeper into Google—beyond the second or third page. Find out what other types of websites your competitor ranks for on those pages, which you might end up ranking for on the first page of Google. Unfortunately Google never gives away its methodologies or algorithms, so the best strategy is to use a "best-guess and shotgun" approach.

What I mean by this is, take a good long look at your competitors' social media pages, and you will certainly find plenty of ideas that you could do to improve your own web pages. For example, on YouTube there is the ability to build out a robust "About" page for any channel you create. Make sure that page has a URL to your home page (a valuable back-link), a full description of your company, and any other pertinent information your prospects might need to see.

More than ever, for businesses both large and small, a LinkedIn page is critical in this day and age. It has become the de facto résumé or overview for those researching online. Look at how often your competition is posting company updates or industry news.

If your industry is one that is prone to customer complaints due to high volume, such as restaurants, publishing, travel and leisure, etc., you will see your competitors on consumer complaint sites as well.

If you discover that your competitor is constantly receiving complaints, this should be your proverbial "canary in the coal mine" warning that your business could be next.

In the next section I will go into detail about how to repair online reputations, but in my experience in the industry, **if you notice that your complaints are going unanswered, you need to act quickly:**

1. Beef up your customer service team with training and customer skills.

2. Resolve customer issues before they get out of your control and the angry customers move to more toxic websites like Pissed Consumer.

3. Look at their complaints as giving you a window into a potential future of your complaining customers as well. What customers complain about tends to have common elements.

3

REPAIRING REPUTATION

EASIER TO IMMUNIZE THAN TO REPAIR

It's far easier to work on immunizing your reputation than it is to repair one that is out of control due to a spiraling number of complaints. Once the genie of negative reviews is out of the bottle, it's difficult to convince that monster to get back into the bottle.

Beyond the benefits repairing your online image have on what people see on search engines, taking concrete steps to prevent complaints in the first place through my suggestions in the "Immunize" section of the book will ultimately mean greater customer satisfaction and stronger brand loyalty.

But if your first few pages of search engines are already scarred by negative reviews—true or untrue—*do not panic*. There are some very real concrete steps that you can take to minimize their impact or indeed remove them completely. Obviously if the reviews are true, you will need to quickly make some big changes, then respond directly.

It is not a three-alarm fire, but certainly owners of both small and large businesses often feel a sense of helplessness when they see their good name and hard-earned reputation being dragged through the mud. Like any fire, if you can get to the crux of the problem quickly, you can stamp it out. If you use the steps I've outlined in my Total Online Reputation system, then you can have the basic tools so you may take full control of positive online messaging.

Not All Complaint Sites Are Equal

> Peter showed the complaints of Dreamy Cupcakes to Maria, who scowled mightily. She leaned forward to look closer, clicked on page 2 of the Google search results, and pointed to a text from Ripoff Report that said "DREAMY CUPCAKES RIPPED ME OFF!" She turned to look at Peter, who bit his lip in dismay.
>
> "Ripoff Report? What on earth is that?" asked Maria.
>
> "I've heard of the site here and there," replied Peter slowly.
>
> "But I have no idea what it is or how it actually works."

Much to the delight of consumers, the Wild West scenario on the internet feeds both the curiosity and the natural inquisitiveness of consumers with a mind-boggling array of choices. Sadly, it also has become the first place to lodge a complaint about a service or product … or a person.

The internet has also spawned a number of websites that give disgruntled consumers a massive platform to vent. This has been a double-edged sword: wary consumers can now research information about a company, but they are also victims of an unedited source of information.

Many businesses have (ironically) complained about complaint sites. Their chief beef is that the comments are not moderated or verified and thus subject to potential lies, unsubstantiated distortions of the truth, or flat-out *fake news.*

Currently the biggest target for businesses' grievances is a site called **RipoffReport.com**. If you're the unfortunate recipient of complaints against yourself or your company on this site, you likely know it all too well.

RipoffReport.com used to rank extraordinarily well on the first page of Google, so much so that it frequently was within the top five listings on page 1. Thus, any tiny complaint on the site would immediately show up when someone was searching for the name of a business, product, or professional.

To make matters worse, there were always grumblings that Ripoff Report.com participated in shady activities, including what's known as "black hat" search engine optimization techniques, to have their pages rank higher on Google.

Numerous lawsuits filed against the company have so far been ineffective. Over the past few years, several high-profile lawsuits have failed because much internet content is protected by the First Amendment.

RepGold Tip:

When doing searches for the purpose of online reputation, open a web browser in Incognito or Privacy mode. (In Google Chrome it is called Incognito.) Other web browsers use different terms. What they all have in common is the ability to conduct searches in a native fashion with all personalized search results stripped out. Google will commonly change your search results based on what you click on. Thus, what Google shows you will be different than its traditional search result. Using Incognito or other privacy browsing options prevents this, giving you a neutral picture of your search results that isn't distorted by your personal web-surfing habits.

Other well-known sites include **ComplaintsBoard.com** and

PissedConsumer.com. Together with **RipoffReport.com**, these make up the Big Three of complaint websites.

The first thing to do is to conduct a careful search on your company's name, your product, your executives, or even your name on Google and see if any one of these sites show up within the first few pages of Google. Now remember that 90 percent of all searchers don't go past the first page of Google, but if indeed there are complaints lodged against you on the first five pages or so, they have the ability to quickly skyrocket up to the first page of Google.

Remember to also do variations of your search by adding in words like "scam," "complaint," "sucks," and the like. See if any complaints are already out there by using different search terms.

Unfortunately the worry doesn't end there. Each industry has its own specific user groups or forums where customers gather online. Take the timeshare industry, for instance: websites such as the Timeshare User Group (TUG) or Redweek are full of forums where people complain, and these sites rank extraordinarily well on Google. If you're a local business, people may complain directly on your Google My Business listing (not good) or on Yelp or Facebook (even worse).

Action Items

1. Visit the Big Three complaint sites (RipoffReport.com, ComplaintsBoard.com, PissedConsumer.com) and do searches for your business or name (make sure you're using a web browser in Incognito or Privacy mode).
2. Search Google for your business or name and see which websites pop up that have good or bad reviews. Make a note of those sites.
3. Search Google for your competitors or related businesses and see which websites pop up that have good or bad reviews. Make a note of those sites.

4. Regularly check Google and those sites (see more info in our chapter on monitoring).

SILVER LINING: KNOWING THE COMPLAINTS AND FACING THE MUSIC OF NEGATIVE ONLINE REVIEWS

> Peter and Maria sat in stony silence. Finally, Maria broke the tension by saying lightheartedly, "Well, at least we know we have a problem." Peter cracked a grin. There was certainly wisdom in Maria's comment.

While finding negative reviews on search engines can be like a punch to the gut, especially if they aren't true or at best are a distortion of the truth, there is a silver lining to the dark cloud.

Think of it this way: Would you rather not know that your customers are unhappy while you struggle to build your business year after year? Would you rather have your head in the sand as you wonder why your sales continue to slide? For the good of your business, you need to hear the truth and face the music … even if it hurts. I will readily admit, it is easier said than done.

Before the explosion of online reviews, bad customer experiences were basically limited to the speed of word of mouth (still quite formidable in itself). But now with the integration of social media in our daily lives, a bad experience can fly across the internet in the click of a mouse and find a permanent home on the first page of Google.

The way to think of it is like disease. If you are diagnosed early, your odds of surviving and recovering are much higher than if you discover it when it's too late. Complaints are like a disease to your business that can sap away its health and vitality until there's nothing left.

In my experience, the rule of thumb is that for every person that complains online, there's likely at least ten times that number of people who are angry at the problem or issue for the same reason. Think about it. How angry does someone have to be to turn on the computer, get on the internet, find a complaint site, create a user account, then type out a long complaint?

Under normal circumstances, most people wouldn't spend the time to do so unless they were very upset. While it's not good news, it's better to find out early before the problem really grows out of control and you can take immediate action.

Action Items

1. Think of online complaints as doing your business a favor.
2. Do *not* ignore online complaints. It can be a signal that there is something seriously wrong.
3. Research the alleged complaints in-depth. Be honest and admit to yourself that the complainer may be right. After all, they did take the time to lodge the complaint on a website.
4. If the complaints are true, aggressively work on resolving the issues. Tell the complainer what you have done to correct the problem or issue.

REALITY CHECK: THE BIGGER YOU ARE ...

The facts are out there in plain sight. The larger a business you own, the more likely there are complaints about you. It's just a matter of numbers. If 2 percent of your customers dislike you, the total number is bound to be more if you have one million customers (20,000) versus if you have one hundred (2).

Consequently, if you are part of a Fortune 500 or worldwide brand, a basic fact of life will be that no matter what you do, many people will not like you. And the larger your business is, the more people dislike you and post complaints online. You simply cannot please everyone. This is true for companies that perpetually rank low on customer service surveys (airlines, wireless providers, cable providers) as well as brands that rank high in customer loyalty.

What this means is that as a large company or large brand, your goal is not the same as that for a small or midsize company or professional.

Big and small businesses are not alike, and the same goes for their customer complaints. For big businesses, the goals are more about "triage" or "management" rather than looking toward online reputation management as a silver bullet or cure. A large company will never be able to fully prevent or eliminate complaints, nor will they be able to satisfy disgruntled customers no matter what lengths they go to.

Perhaps in the future the ORM industry will need to generate statistics for companies called "reputation churn." If the statistics are within an acceptable boundary of a preestablished reputation churn, then that is manageable. If the numbers soar outside the boundaries, then warnings and numbers need to be examined and drastic action taken.

The reason why some amount of churn isn't of a huge concern to a big company is that as long as their growth rate exceeds their churn rate, net growth will keep things moving forward. For example, if they lose five customers a month but gain twenty-five, their net growth is twenty. So it may be with your reputation churn. As you grow, as long as your positive reputation points online far outweigh the inevitable negative reviews, your overall reputation will continue to improve.

That's not to say that a large company or brand cannot benefit from any of the strategies and tactics outlined in this book. On the contrary, implementing many of the ideas and action items here can help strengthen brand loyalty while reducing exposure to reputation churn.

Action Items
- Do a reality check. Is your company so large or does it conduct business so frequently that it isn't realistic to completely

eliminate online negative reviews? If so, view online reputation management as an ongoing normal part of business rather than a cure.

WHAT NOT TO DO

> Peter set his face in a determined grimace and started to click and type.
>
> "What are you doing?" asked Maria.
>
> "It's obvious this review is completely biased and doesn't tell the whole story," Peter muttered. "I'm going to give this guy a piece of my mind and show people that we don't take well to lies."
>
> Maria put her hand gently on Peter's. "I really don't think getting into an online argument is something that will help."
>
> Peter's face started to relax and he thought about it. "Perhaps you're right...."

Almost as important as knowing how to proactively try to fix a bad situation is understanding what *not* to do that could make a bad review or complaint much worse. This will not only hinder your repair efforts but could seriously damage your reputation among customers. Make sure to carefully review these points and provide them to your marketing and customer service team. Educating your employees is critical to ensure that these mistakes aren't made.

Don't Get Into a Lengthy Back-and-Forth Argument

The internet is perfect for fostering online conversations. But it can also sometimes be a hostile place. Message board threads and comment threads can go on and on with people posting their opinions and replying to negative posts.

When faced with a customer complaint or a reviewer who is lying, it is often tempting to try to set the record straight. After all, you want to make sure that your point is being made and you don't want the complainer to perpetuate falsehoods or misconceptions.

However, one of the worst things you can do is to get into a lengthy back-and-forth argument online with a complainer. There are three surprising but commonsense reasons for this:

1. First and foremost, these actions can actually backfire and keep that negative web page ranked high on Google. In some cases, posting constantly on that one thread will actually *boost* the page higher on Google, creating a new problem that may have the completely opposite effect than desired. Google is constantly ranking web pages that have a high view count in relevant content and also freshness of content. Thus, all things being equal, a web page with a couple of negative posts from two years ago will rank much lower than a web page with a high volume of posts every other day. Every time you respond to a complaint with a volley of posts, the higher the website ranks.

2. It looks bad. While you may feel the need to rebut the complainer and respond to each of his complaints, in many ways that constant back-and-forth can look unprofessional. Other readers may find it to be defensive and argumentative. And the more you post, the greater the chance that you will eventually say (type) things you'll later regret. **Remember, what you type on the Internet has a shelf life of** *forever.*

3. It is likely ineffective. Some complaints are legitimate and can be resolved. But sadly, there is a growing group of consumers who use these complaint and rip-off websites just to see their names posted, and it can quickly become very toxic. For this group, there is virtually and literally nothing you can do to placate their nastiness. Therefore, going back and forth

with them will do nothing but provoke them to write even more negative posts.

How to Deal with Negative Posts and/or Bad Reviews

Now that I've told you why you shouldn't exacerbate an argument, what *should* you do?

- Keep your reply to one post. No matter how tempting it is, keep it to one post. One post!
- Summarize your position and clarify the situation using facts, data, and logic. Online arguments tend to devolve into a he-said/she-said situation, full of passion and emotion. Just stick to the facts.
- Keep your tone polite and somewhat formal. You can disagree with someone while still being polite.

Following the above steps will keep the negative post from becoming constantly fresh content (which Google loves), it will make you sound professional and courteous, and it will provide an avenue for the aggrieved to contact someone.

Action Items

1. Post a reply once and only once. Stick to the facts and offer another means for the complainer to contact you.
2. Remember, avoid getting into a heated back-and-forth. It will hurt you by helping keep that post high on Google rankings.

Insider Tip:

Provide an email address or a business phone number that the disgruntled consumer can use to try to resolve the situation if needed.

ORM GUERILLA TACTICS
HOW TO TAKE DOWN COMPLAINTS PERMANENTLY ... FOREVER, PART 1

Offer Freebies

In my experience, one of the most highly effective means to make a complainer happy is to offer something in return to make things right. For example, if you are in a hospitality business, it could be a free night's stay or two. Perhaps a free upgrade to the best suite or free resort credits. In businesses such as travel and leisure, plan to give away something that will not cost you anything ... an empty hotel room for example.

If you're an electronics company, you can offer to replace the faulty product for a new one. If the price point is too high, offer a credit for your products.

Smaller local businesses can offer free meals, free service, free any-thing that will make the customer happy. It is a good business plan, as your most ardent complainer may just delete the negative post and give you a positive review instead.

RepGold Tip:
An important note to remember is to do your best to offer freebies in private, *not* on the public message board of the complaint.

Offer the customer something in exchange for them taking down their entire complaint. Most complaint sites or message boards allow the original poster to delete their thread (not all of them, Complaints-Board.com being a notable exception). You can see the benefits here if they delete the complaint thread:

1. It will permanently remove the listing from Google.

2. It will ideally remove all the subsequent replies if they include people that agree with the complainer.
3. It saves you a ton of SEO work trying to "push down" the negative review.

Please make sure that this negotiation is not done in public, such as online or using social media that everyone can see. Ideally it should be done over the phone. This avoids having it being seen *by the public* because it could be misconstrued as you bribing the complainer to take down his posting. This direct action will prevent copycats from taking advantage of your generosity and then posting more negative online complaints in an attempt to cash in on free goodies.

The ORM Detective Work:
Contacting the Negative Online Poster

This information is generally available to the public. There are no shortcuts, and often administrators are very protective of giving their users' information to another party. These solutions vary from website to website. If in doubt, you can email the site administrator to find out about their rules. For sites such as YouTube, you can email the user who posts videos by looking for their contact information if they have an About tab. If it is a private blog, more detective work will be required, including using WhoIs.com to try to find out who the owner of the domain is if they don't respond or don't have a Contact Me link. Try Googling their name + "LinkedIn" to see if they have a profile there. If so, and if you have an upgraded account, you can

> **RepGold Tip:**
> WhoIs.com is a handy tool to find out who a website is registered to. Sometimes that info is directly blocked, or sometimes it will only have the info of the domain registrar, but sometimes it will have the actual person's address and email.

use LinkedIn's InMail system to directly contact them.

Here's a sample email to send to the complainer:

Dear <INSERT NAME>,

I'm very sorry to hear that you were unhappy with your latest purchase of our _____. At <INSERT COMPANY NAME> we really do care about your satisfaction and want to try to make things right.

Would you be open to accepting a free replacement product? If after you receive the product and it's to your satisfaction, we only ask that you please remove your complaint.

If this works for you, please reply with a shipping address that we can send your free replacement product to.

Thanks in advance.

Now you're probably asking, what's to stop them from taking the free product and not deleting the complaint? The answer is nothing. But nothing ventured, nothing gained; you do not have anything to lose, and the payoff can be tremendous if they do permanently delete it. Having a negative review deleted rather than having to spend the time to push it down on search engine results pages can save you a year of work and tens of thousands of dollars.

In social psychology, the official term for this is "norm of reciprocity." The norm of reciprocity is the social expectation that people will respond to each other in kind—returning benefits for benefits. In other words, if you give them something for free, they will feel compelled to return the favor by doing what you asked them to do.

I have used these exact methods to take down some of the most egregious offenders from the first page of Google. And all it cost was a free product or service here and there.

Here's a quick success story to share with you. I had a client who sold security cameras. The company in question was shocked when they learned that there was a terrible negative review posted on a YouTube video clip.

The fact that it was a video made it doubly bad because it drove home how bad the product was. The Google ranking was also very high on the first page, and whenever a customer searched the company name, the offensive review was always lurking on page 1.

The solution we came up with was to email the consumer and offer to send the latest and greatest camera in exchange for removing the offending video. The camera was sent, we followed up with the client, and eventually the video was taken down and disappeared from Google forever.

It's truly a win-win method. The disgruntled consumer is now a happy camper. He may spread the word on how great the company's customer service is and go from being a hater to an evangelist. Permanently deleting a negative review from the first page of Google saves you an untold amount of work, money, and lost business.

Action Items

1. Find out how you can directly and privately contact the complainer on the website.
2. Email them an offer to make things right in exchange for permanently deleting the complaint.
3. Always follow up.

HOW TO TAKE DOWN COMPLAINTS PERMANENTLY ... FOREVER, PART 2

If your efforts to negotiate or contact negative posters in part 1 fail or are not possible, there are other options. The tactics in part 1 have a high degree of success, and as I mentioned before, nothing ventured, nothing gained. If the overall goal is to repair and maintain your reputation, the best solution is getting the negative reviews removed from a website permanently. These steps are worth a try and in the long term may save your business money and headaches.

ASK SITE TO TAKE DOWN
DUE TO INACCURATE INFO

If the consumer complaint is a blatant lie, and you have proof, there's no harm in contacting the website owner and asking them to take down the information due to completely inaccurate information or falsehoods. The worst that can happen is they ignore you or say no. If you persist, you may make some headway and convince their editor that you are justified. Most website owners care about their reputations and wouldn't want something on their site to remain if it was proven to be a lie.

ASK SITE TO TAKE DOWN
USING ADVERTISING AS LEVERAGE

Another tactic worth trying is to use future advertising as leverage to get the website owner to take down the content. Here's how it would work.

Contact their Advertising or Sales contact if they have one or the webmaster if they don't. Inquire about direct advertising opportunities on their website. Many sites these days don't bother with direct sales of online ads, instead choosing to go with ad networks such as Google AdSense, AdChoices, or Taboola. But some still do directly sell online ad spaces.

RepGold Tip:
Back up your request with as much factual data as you have. And as is the case in public postings, keep your emails to editors or webmasters at these sites as polite as possible.

Negotiate a basic introductory package of online ads. When they send you the Insertion Order to sign and seal the deal, email them that

you noticed there was web content on their site mentioning your business in a negative light. Due to that fact, you wouldn't be comfortable advertising on their site until it was taken down. Larger websites may have a strict separation between sales and editorial, but smaller sites would rather pocket the profit and just take down the content.

Make the determination of the cost benefit of spending money on the ads in exchange for removing the offending content. If it means getting rid of it from the first page of Google, it could be well worth it.

Reminder: Always keep your end of the bargain and buy the advertising space if they agree to take the ad down, lest they just repost the negative content.

THREATEN LEGAL ACTION

If the postings are particularly egregious and harmful, potentially revealing confidential information, you may wish to consult with an attorney to see what your legal options are in terms of pressuring the website to remove the offending content.

> Disclaimer: Please note that I am not a lawyer, and nothing I recommend in this book is from a legal perspective. When it comes to legal action or activities, always consult an appropriate legal professional first.

Please keep in mind that this avenue has a low rate of success. Websites are generally protected by a law called the Communications Decency Act, which protects sites with user-generated content.[7] Still, some smaller sites may just decide that it is easier to take down the content rather than engage in lengthy and costly litigation. Even the threat of litigation may be enough to get it taken down. But you better be sure you really have been harmed. Filing baseless libel suits are known as SLAPPs—strategic lawsuits against public participation can backfire.

---

[7] https://www.eff.org/issues/cda230

Many business owners frustrated with false accusations against them decide they have been "slandered." In a legal context, definitions matter. *Slander* is a false spoken statement, meaning verbal. *Libel* is a published false statement that is damaging to a person's reputation.

Others have taken their frustrations out by suing the actual negative reviewers, as is the case of a dentist by the name of Nima Dayani who sued five patients for damages ranging from $50,000 to $100,000. Consider this option with great caution. Generally speaking, it's not a wise business practice to be known for suing your previous customers.

Still other businesses have started to add what are called "gag clauses" in agreements where customers unknowingly sign away their rights to post online reviews after making a purchase of a product or service. To be very clear, I do not recommend this action as it seems like cutting your nose off to spite your face.

In any event, you may wish to read the Communications Decency Act before making any threats of litigation. You may also wish to really determine if you are in the right or if you have actual legal standing. Legal action is never fun, and it is usually costly and stressful. Be sure to weigh the costs and benefits, and again, make sure to consult with a qualified legal professional first.

Action Items

1. Contact the website and provide your reason for them to take down their complaint *or* ask for advertising rates and threaten to pull your purchase if they don't take it down.
2. Remain polite and professional as you make your case.
3. If the posting is extremely damaging or malicious, consider the legal option after speaking with a legal professional.

The Case of Ripoff Report

The highest-profile consumer complaint site, Ripoff Report, has long been a thorn in the side of many businesses due to the fact that for some time their complaints ranked high on search engines.

Ripoff Report has been protected by the courts despite an onslaught of legal challenges. Their policy of not allowing even the original authors of complaints to remove their postings led to a 2007 lawsuit that eventually was found in favor of Ripoff Report, wherein the court found that indeed they were not required to remove complaints.

Companies have also tried to take down complaints by suing the posters of the complaints themselves and obtaining injunctions that required the removal of the offending materials. The courts' decisions have generally upheld that Ripoff Report did not have to comply with the injunctions although a Florida state court reached the opposite conclusion.

Long story short, a whole host of lawsuits have really gone nowhere against Ripoff Report in this area.

What really concerned businesses was not merely the posting of customer complaints but allegations that the owner was engaged in a form of extortion. Ripoff Report had a program called "Corporate Advocacy, Business Remediation & Customer Satisfaction Program" where you paid a fee and the site may, after investigation, change the title to reflect that a company had joined the program. None of the court challenges of extortion have been successful to date.

Before you think about calling up your attorney to sue Ripoff Report, keep in mind that Ripoff Report has actually been successful with "SLAPP-back" lawsuits where they countersue plaintiffs, with one such case being found in favor of Ripoff Report in May 2011. You can find out the latest news on Ripoff Report by just checking them out on Wikipedia.org.

More recently, listings from Ripoff Report don't rank quite so high on Google, to the delight of many companies and search engine optimization firms who had long complained to Google about the website and some allegedly question-able tactics they used to rank high.

 The battle involving Ripoff Report looks to continue una-bated and provides a fascinating look at the evolution of law and how it applies to a relatively new medium such as the internet. The implications go beyond just legal findings and may end up impacting your business in a material way, so it would behoove you to stay up-to-date on the findings.

4

Short-Term Tactics to Repair Reputation

So your worst nightmare is realized. Just like Peter and Maria and their Dreamy Cupcakes business, you type in your business name, your name, or your product's name and on the first page of a major search engine you see one or more complaints. Your blood turns to ice and a rivulet of sweat trickles down your brow. The thought of your prospective customers reading the complaint makes your stomach churn. Fear not, as there are some things you can do to immediately counter the negativity.

One of the advantages of trying to rank certain items high on search engines for your own company name is that there shouldn't be much competition (unless your name or company name is shared by other companies). Even if that is the case, unless other companies with the same name have listings on the first page of Google that are on pages with really strong SEO factors that make Google like it, you still have a good shot at leapfrogging their listings and ranking higher.

RUN GOOGLE "PAY PER CLICK" ADS IMMEDIATELY

The fastest and surest way to get your message onto Google is to run ads through their Google AdWords program. Known as "pay per click," or PPC, AdWords didn't invent this format of advertising, but due to the dominance of the Google search engine, it is by far the largest PPC player. Ads on Google's search results page are usually in stacks of three, both at the top of the page and at the bottom. They are distinguished from the "organic" or natural search results by the little tag that says "Ad" by the listing.

For those who are familiar with AdWords, simply create a few new campaigns using keywords that include the name in question that generates the negative search results. You will need to use three different AdWords accounts, which will require three different email addresses. This way, all three ads will show simultaneously.

Your headline and ad copy can focus on positive news, corporate communication positioning, or recent news. And unless you're a large and well-known brand, most likely no one else is really bidding on your name as a keyword, so the cost-per-click and budget required should be quite low.

Google's AdWords program is dead easy to get started and run ads. You can find out more info at adwords.google.com. There are often coupons that even give you dollars off for new AdWords accounts that can be found with a quick search online or even a call to Google's ad department.

Follow the simple steps to get your account set up. The most important part is to make sure to use the name in question in Keywords. For instance, in Peter and Maria's case, the keywords they would use include variations on "Dreamy Cupcakes." They might include "Dreamy Cupcakes," "reviews for Dreamy Cupcakes," "Dreamy Cupcake complaints," and other similar ones.

If all else fails and you are struggling with getting it set up, contact a search engine marketing expert or contact our sister agency Firecracker PR to let us help you with a comprehensive repair program.

The way search engine PPC ad systems work is that when someone searches a company's name, if you had entered your company name as one of the keywords in AdWords, a text ad may appear on the top of the search results page. Thus, you have a direct

RepGold Tip:

Running three different Google Ad-Words campaigns at the same time has another benefit. Sometimes two or three of the ads will show at the very top of the search results page, thereby pushing down all the other potentially negative organic search results. Since research shows that most searchers don't go beyond what's "above the fold" (meaning what you can see on a web page without having to scroll down), your Ad-Words ads may very well bump the negative search result below the fold, thereby decreasing the number of searchers who see it and click on it.

and simple way to immediately get your message out to try to counter the negative listing.

WRITE AND DISTRIBUTE A PRESS RELEASE

A press release is simply a public notification written in a certain format that is then distributed via a wire service. This makes your press release "live." Although changes to Google have lessened the impact of press releases, they still can rank relatively well for a short period of time directly off of the wire service website.

Sometimes other websites will be interested in your press release and pick up the news, running it word for word on their site. If those websites are relatively well regarded by search engines, you can have your news with your name rank higher on Google.

Writing effective press releases isn't all that difficult, but neither should it be taken too lightly. After all, when it goes out it is made public pretty much forever. So make sure to watch what you say, and always have someone proofread it before sending it out.

RepGold Tip:
Here are some tips to write effective and powerful press releases:

- Make sure you have something interesting to say. While you can announce a new executive hire or mention that your company will be exhibiting at an upcoming trade show, the best use of a press release is to generate excitement. Use it to launch a new product or new promotion. How about doing a survey and publishing the results? Or try testing a contest on Facebook or your own website.

- Include the name you are trying to repair in the headline of the press release. It is the headline that will show as the title of any listing on search engines, so it's crucial that your company name/product name/personal name is in the title and ideally near the front of the headline.

- When writing a press release, use the "inverted pyramid" method. Stack all the most important information up front and leave all the least important details toward the end. This is a bit counterintuitive for those used to writing reports in college, but it's critical in press releases. The media gets bombarded with press releases and only has time to quickly scan the headline and maybe the first paragraph. You need to make sure all the essential info is front-loaded.

- Use the who, when, why, where, what method when writing your release. Who is going to read the release? When is the announcement happening? Why are you offering a press release? Where, if applicable? What is the news?
- Press releases use a certain format and structure. Read some press releases from companies in your industry to get a feel for it. Make sure to stick to the right tone of voice and writing format.
- This sounds basic, but double- and triple-check your spelling and grammar. Do not simply rely on your word processor's spell-check program; it can't tell if "tired" or "tried" is what you mean, and both will seem correct to it. Have someone else proofread your release—you are always going to be your own worst proofreader.
- Lower your expectations. As I mentioned above, the media gets bombarded with hundreds of press releases, the majority of which are of no interest to them. Do not expect to get much, if any, press in major outlets by just sending out a press release. The most you can hope for is for the wire service posting to get picked up by search engines, or for a more niche website to run it word for word and it ends up ranking well.
- Choose the right wire service to put your press release on. The plethora of choices can be confusing, and they rank from very cheap to extremely expensive.

If your writing skills are not great, don't hesitate to outsource the writing. You can look for freelance writers on sites such as Upwork. For those in need of full-blown public relations campaigns beyond simple press releases, contact our sister agency FirecrackerPR.com.

How to Create Social Media Profiles

As social media websites have grown in size and variety, their relevance to searchers is rewarded by search engines with a high ranking for branded names. During the dawn of social media, sites such as Friendster and MySpace were the de facto standard. But the rise and dominance of Facebook, Twitter, LinkedIn, and other sites have caused different social media sites to rank high with varying degrees.

RepGold Tip:
Stay up-to-date on the latest "hot" websites. Type in the names of some of your bigger competitors and see which social media sites come up on page 1.

It is a good bet that creating a profile page for your own name, your company name, or your brand name will have some success in seeing it ranked high on search engines. In 2018 when this book was written, the better-known social media websites to target include:

- Facebook
- Twitter
- LinkedIn
- Instagram
- Pinterest
- Tumblr

The obvious caveat to the above list is that the relevance and even the existence of many of these sites may come and go relative to the blinding speed of the internet.

If your personal name or business name is common or shared by several others, you may find it difficult to have it rank higher on search engines like Google. To combat this issue, add as much relevant information within the profile section of the social media sites as possible, including links to your other websites, pictures, videos, and the like. Google's constant revisions to their search engine formula will continue to place a high importance on relevance and a diversity of content forms.

Similar to our tips on why you shouldn't engage in a back-and-forth online debate on a complaint-website posting, it can be helpful to have social media sites that are active with tweets, postings, comments, and other activities. In essence, all things being equal, search engines like websites (social media or otherwise) that have fresh and constant postings.

RepGold Tip:
For businesses, particularly those in technology or other emerging spaces, make sure to add your company to Crunchbase. Their directory is quickly becoming a top directory website that also ranks extremely well on Google.

"Link building" for your social media profiles is another way to improve your chances of higher-ranking pages. Seek out a search engine optimization (SEO) firm or contact Firecracker PR for link-building services.

LOCAL OR BUSINESS DIRECTORIES

Website directories serve two purposes. The first is to get your website greater visibility among people looking for your product or service. The second is to help your SEO rankings of the target website.

Google's authoritative voice on all things SEO, Matt Cutts, had previously named three specific directories that Google values highly: *Yahoo! Paid Directory*, *Business.com*, and *Best of the Web*. Besides being directories that have high authority, another reason they are looked upon favorably by Google is that they all require annual payments to be listed, in the range of $299 per year per directory. As you can see, purchasing listings with just these three directories alone could cost a hefty amount and thus discourage websites that aren't serious about their endeavor (particularly "black hat" SEO types).

For online reputation management purposes where you might be trying to push ten or more of your domains higher in the rankings, this could prove problematic. Of course if money is no object, try to purchase directory listings for each of your sites. A decent fallback position is to select one of them only; my choice would be Yahoo!

In the ever-expanding and ever-changing online world, always make sure our information is still applicable by doing a bit of your own online searching.

Depending on the specific industry, there should be a handful of other directories that you can find suitable to your audience. Google your industry plus "directory," "directories," "associations," "listings," and other variations to see what's out there.

GOOGLE MY BUSINESS

For local businesses, it goes without saying that you absolutely need to be listed with Google My Business (formerly known as Google Places). Searching for a business name, if it is listed with Google My Business, the website will bring up a search result that has a blurb about the business, some detailed information, and a small picture of a map if the business has a physical presence.

The goal is to stack the first page of Google with as many listings that you control as possible. A Google My Business listing receives a prominent placement near the top of the search results and also takes up quite a bit of space to boot. Since research shows that 90 percent of searchers don't look below the first five search results, the more space you can take up "above the fold" the better.

The Google My Business listing may also trigger a Google map to appear or an information box on the right-hand side that pulls information from various sources (known as the Google Knowledge Graph).

There is no way to control whether or not Google chooses to display the Knowledge Graph. But you can maximize your odds by making sure your listing is as robust as possible. Local businesses need to make sure their Google My Business listing is accurate and complete. At a minimum, all the information about your business should be entered. Going above and beyond by adding more photos, a video if possible, and encouraging your customers to post positive reviews on your listing will certainly help your cause.

One of the trickiest parts of Google My Business is the verification process. This involves both adding a new listing as well as claiming an existing listing that Google has already pre-populated. As expected, Google will want to verify that you are who you say you are. They offer two ways to verify your information: phone and mail.

The preferred method to get verified is by phone because it's faster and more accurate. However, it's important to note that the phone number they will call you at is the one you list on Google My Business. Therefore, if you have an automated phone system with extensions, it is going to be very difficult to get verified by phone. Don't use your cell phone number to get verified unless you want that to be your main contact number that everyone in the world sees. When you do confirm you want to use phone verification, be close by to answer and jot down the PIN code.

RepGold Tip:
From an SEO point of view, it's not widely known that you can do link building for Google My Business listings to get them to show up higher when prospects search for certain keywords. Use the Google Keyword Tool to find which keywords your prospects search for, then make sure to include those phrases in your description.

If phone verification is not an option, the only other means is via a postcard in the mail. The time to receive it could be weeks, and the risk of having the postcard thrown out mistakenly as junk mail is real. Ask your receptionist or whoever accepts the mail to be on the lookout for it.

Note that because Google is always evolving, the methods I've listed here may have changed by the time you read this. Be sure to check Google's options for verification.

Here are the simple steps to find out what the URL on Google My Business is to do link building for:

Step 1: Do a search for your business name and click on the Google My Business link. It should take you to a page dedicated to your location.

Step 2: Click on the icon that says "Share."

Step 3: Copy the entire URL string and paste it in Word or some other text-editing program (even email would work). For my agency, Firecracker PR, it is

https://goo.gl/maps/zxz6qNEVBkQ2.

Voilà! This is the URL for this particular Google My Business listing.

YouTube

Google also owns YouTube, so it goes without saying that YouTube videos can rank well and often make it onto the first page of Google. Because of the potential real estate a block of YouTube videos can comprise on the first page, it is well worth your time to create and upload a video.

Tools such as Camtasia Studio are invaluable for whipping up videos

RepGold Tip:
To maximize your potential for ranking the video high for your name, make sure to follow these tips:

quickly and easily using nothing more than a PowerPoint presentation. Don't fret about making a perfect video. When time is of the essence, create anything you can for now.

- Name the actual video file using your name. For instance, if the video file is automatically going to be saved as file1256.mov, rename it YourCompany.mov (replace "Your-Company" with the name of the person, product, or company you're doing ORM for).
- Include the name in the title of the video, as well as in the description. Most people skimp on the description, but you can actually copy and paste the entire script of the video into the description. Aside from ORM benefits, the long tail keywords in the script may very well help you rank for SEO purposes.
- Create a "channel" for your brand using your name. This will give you a dedicated page for your videos that have a URL in the format of http://youtube.com/yourbrand. As Google likes URLs with target keywords in them, this gives your channel a good chance to rank high on Google as well.
- Ask people to subscribe to your channel. Subscriptions seem to be a key factor in video ranking.
- Promote your video where you can to get people to Like it and comment on it. The line of thought is, the more active the reviews for a video, the higher it may potentially rank. You may want to look at giving your video a kick-start by going to a site such as Fiverr.com to find people who will Like YouTube videos.

In terms of link building for YouTube videos, as with the publication of this book, the consensus seems to be that this action can definitely help your ranking of the video within the YouTube site itself. However, it doesn't seem to do anything in terms of making it more or less likely that the video will appear on Google's general search results. Please keep in mind that, with all things Google, the effectiveness of these strategies and tactics may vary and can change in a heartbeat. The best bet is to stay up-to-date with all the search engine industry's happenings on a site such as SEOmoz.org.

Online reputation management tactics can and will vary, but this option also offers you an opportunity to present your company or products and services in a compelling way. Don't neglect the other side of the coin in pursuit of higher rankings for maintaining positive ranking and protecting your brand.

Online Classifieds

An easier and cheaper solution can be using classified websites such as Craigslist to throw up an ad that has the name you are trying to protect in the title and description. But because most ads have a time limit on how long they are posted, it is debatable how beneficial they are for ORM. Considering it takes only a few minutes to create a classified ad, you might as well create it and see how it ranks.

RepGold Tip:

Another advanced strategy that has not been proven to a degree of certainty (but couldn't hurt) is using Google's feature of adding closed captioning. As this is just more text that Google can glean information from, adding closed-captioning to the video may give your video a further boost in rankings. To find out more details on how to do this, Google "how to add closed captioning to YouTube video" and follow any number of instructions.

5

LONG-TERM TACTICS TO REPAIR AND IMMUNIZE REPUTATION

SUSTAINED PUBLIC RELATIONS

One of the surefire ways to maintain, build, and guard online reputation and keep it golden is through public relations. If PR is done consistently, with a real plan, the additional benefits include more awareness of your product or service and possibly increased sales.

PR is often misunderstood by those outside the industry, just as many people automatically think that "marketing" means "advertising" and nothing else. In my experience most think "PR" only means "press release."

In fact the press release is *one* tool in the toolkit of a complete public relations plan. As I've mentioned previously, the press release is an essential part of an overall plan, but like any good carpenter, no single tool can actually complete a job properly. Generating positive press coverage can have a huge effect on your online reputation management efforts.

Google particularly loves websites with high authority, and most of the well-known media websites fall directly into that category. It goes without saying that a positive story about your company in the local newspaper, tech blog, industry magazine, or any other influential media outlet can dramatically impact the way people perceive of your business.

That is why there has been a growing trend toward a greater focus on PR and less reliance on traditional advertising. One groundbreaking book in this regard is *The Fall of Advertising and the Rise of PR* by Al Ries and Laura Ries (HarperCollins Publishers, 2004). Their theory is that public relations is superior in building brands from the ground up, while advertising excels in maintaining supremacy of existing top brands. The book provides ample real-world case studies to back up their claims.

While this book is mainly concerned with maintaining and repairing online reputation, it isn't my intention to provide a comprehensive instruction manual of creating and implementing a public relations strategy. There are plenty of books that do a much better job than we could ever do. Two starter books that will set you on the right path include *Public Relations Kit for Dummies* by Eric Yaverbaum (Wiley, 2001) and *Full Frontal PR* by Richard Laermer (Wiley, 2004).

However, since PR can be so powerful in creating and maintaining a positive online reputation, I will spend some time delving into various activities of public relations as it directly pertains to reputation management.

PR has a dual benefit of both repairing your reputation as well as immunizing it against future attacks. One of our clients witnessed this firsthand when their reputation was assaulted by a disgruntled foreign company that took offense at a particular business deal that wasn't consummated. The offending party went on Twitter and created false accounts for the purpose of slandering our client, as well as posted lies about their business on other websites.

Luckily our client was already wisely invested in a long-term and consistent PR program for the year or so preceding the attacks, and as a result, none of the negative results showed up on the first page of Google.

Instead, their first page was filled with high-quality search results, including an award they won with a prestigious technology magazine, product reviews on another tech site, an article on another well-known B2B technology website, a press release reprint on CBS MarketWatch, and our client's active social media sites. These results prove that the real power of PR is the best line of defense to protect your online reputation.

Chapter 8 will delve deeper into actual public relations tactics that you can use. Our sister agency Firecracker PR also specializes in creating full-scale media relations campaigns.

Purchase Custom URLs

One of the many factors Google looks at to determine how to rank a website is the URL. Thus, one strategy is to purchase the URLs that include the name you are looking to protect, including hyphenated versions or including words like "blog," "forum," etc. Typically you should purchase the .com, .org, and .net names. Depending on your situation, you may also want to preemptively purchase URLs with your name and the words "sucks," "hate," and other common slanderous words. This may seem counterintuitive or even ridiculous, but it adds another layer of security to maintain your reputation. Website addresses (or domain names as they are typically called) can be purchased from quite a few places, including GoDaddy.

The cost of keeping that website address is about $10 per year, not much money in the grand scheme of things. Make a note on whether the URL is set to automatically renew or if you manually have to pay to renew. It's a bad feeling to have a website you own vanish because the domain name expired.

How to Build Quality, Content-Rich Sites

Peter and Maria's business continued to build a strong following. What they discovered over time was that some of their most loyal customers also enjoyed throwing parties. Maria knew a lot about parties from her days working as a caterer. They decided to create a new website called "Dreamy Cupcake's Ultimate Party Guide." Everything from planning, venue, food selection, music, and, of course, dessert were covered. What initially started out as a labor of love, similar to their cupcake store, soon began attracting a lot of web traffic.

Now that you own domain names with your name in them, it's time to think about building them out into actual websites that can have a high ranking. If the goal of these websites is purely for online reputation purposes, then the sites should be designed with that in mind.

The best way to approach this is to have different themes around each domain name and new website. Having themes will help immensely in content writing and the design. In days past, all you needed to have sites rank high on Google was to stuff your target keywords in the

RepGold Tip:
Don't write content for Google, write for people. In other words, don't write content for the purpose of trying to game Google's system for higher rankings. Rather, write informative and educational content that serves a purpose and that readers find useful and interesting. Having different themes with different target audiences will ensure that the purpose of the website drives the user experience.

Title and Meta tags, then load up on content that repeats your name multiple times. Those days are gone. Instead, Google looks at your website in its entirety, design included. Writing "nonsense" content with repeated keywords doesn't work either. Google's algorithm is such that only good, quality content is looked upon favorably. "Thin" content that doesn't add value just doesn't rank well.

If the thought of building out many websites sounds expensive, it doesn't have to be. Freelance websites such as Upwork.com, Peopleperhour.com, and Freelancer.com have a multitude of web designers who can rely on templates such as WordPress to quickly and easily create impressive-looking websites. Once they are created, you can go in and add content yourself.

There are also do-it-yourself website-building options such as Wix or WordPress. They are fine for simple websites with mostly text, but for more challenging formats, you may wish to hire a designer.

Google also looks very favorably upon websites rich in interactivity. Think of implementing things such as polls, videos, quizzes, a Google Maps snippet, and a message board. Basically think of what you, as a website visitor, would find useful.

Another factor to keep in mind is that Google likes websites with fresh, new content. Thus, having a schedule to write new web pages or blog entries can come in handy. Having RSS feeds that draw in content or Twitter posts is another way to keep things fresh.

Here are some examples of websites you could create:

Official blog. This is a no-brainer. The tougher question is whether the official blog should be integrated into the main website or built as a standalone site. The answer depends on where your priorities lie. If the more important goal is to improve the SEO rankings of the main website, then it may be more valuable to have fresh, relevant blog content on the site itself. However, if immunizing and protecting the online reputation is more important, having a standalone site that may rank and take up a precious slot on the first page of search results is invaluable.

Official forum. Forums are a fantastic way to kill two birds with one stone. One benefit of forums is giving voice to your customers, which is always a good thing. Here, you can interact with your customers and answer their questions or concerns. The second benefit that is more important from an online reputation point of view is that you are funneling complaints from sites such as Pissed Consumer or Ripoff Report, into a site that you control. Part of Google's rankings is based on frequency and volume, so anything you can do to reduce the amount of posts those negative sites get is a good thing. Proboards is one of the leaders in private labeled message boards. Remember to answer questions and complaints quickly and fairly. If someone posts a nasty comment or complaint, respond, resolve it, leave the post up for a while, then delete it. That prevents it from showing up on Google's search engine.

Job listings. If your company is large enough, why not create a standalone website that posts the latest job openings, along with information about why your company is a great place to work? You can also have information on how interested applicants can submit for consideration if they are interested. Other information that can be posted includes any employment policies such as equal opportunity employer, company statistics, etc.

Charity or philanthropy. Why not protect your search engine reputation, improve your actual reputation, and do some good work all at once? There's no better way to do this than through charitable activities. Philanthropy is a fantastic way to help yourself while helping others. On the simple end of the scale, you can create a standalone site that outlines all the charitable activities you're involved in such as charity auctions or events, replete with pictures. Slightly more complicated would be creating some sort of a charity award or competition (remember to put the brand name you want to protect in the name of the award). Higher up on the scale would be to create a scholarship under the person or company's brand name, then promote that scholarship to all the various relevant educational websites. The possibilities are endless. Don't forget to promote your good works to the press. Getting local, industry, or national coverage is another awesome tactic to stack the first page with positive news stories.

Multiple locations. Does your business have multiple locations? Perhaps you can create standalone websites for each location. For example, a hotel resort chain might have six different locations: New England, Quebec City, Miami, Cabo San Lucas, Bermuda, and Vancouver. Websites could be created with the brand name and location name in the URL itself. Information on the cities or regions can be provided. You could also add in location-specific widgets such as a weather widget or a live Twitter feed from that location's tourism board. Important contact information is another possible page. Don't forget the history of the region, top restaurants, and other facts you think your visitors might find valuable.

Games. "Gamification" is all the rage these days. That's just a fancy way of saying, "using games to achieve certain business goals." Almost any brand can benefit from a game, even ones that are business-to-business. Flash-based or Java-based games can be created without spending much. Once again, Upwork or any contractor site should be full of experienced game creators.

E-commerce. Why not create and sell branded products online? Not only might those sites rank well on the first page, but it helps you spread your brand. For instance, In-n-Out Burger sells T-shirts. Many promotional-product companies exist solely to help you stamp your brand on any product imaginable. Create a simple e-commerce website for those products, and voilà, you have another powerful standalone website!

Link Building

In 2016 a major study was published on Brian Dean's excellent Backlinko blog (www.backlinko.com). Of one million Google search results, Dean found that the number of domains linking to a page correlated with rankings more than any other factor. His data also found that a site's overall link authority strongly correlates with higher rankings as well.

This means that a big part of online reputation management is working to increase the rankings of websites you control; link building will inevitably play a major role in your efforts.

What is link building? It's pretty much what the term says: building links. A link from any other website to your site is measured by Google as part of their search formula. But not all links are created equal. Links from important websites, or those with high authority, are weighted more heavily than a link from, say, an unknown website. Still, some links are better than none at all.

Link building as a strategy has been confused with "black hat" SEO, meaning tactics that are frowned upon strongly by Google. But any website over time will accrue links that point to that site naturally. Good link building is basically accelerating those links to improve a website's ranking. Yes, the best type of back-links are those that occur naturally.

For the purposes of online reputation management, especially if you are desperately trying to repair a negative online reputation, you may not have the luxury of time to nurture natural links.

This is where link building comes in. All sorts of providers exist to help build links. The vast majority of them are located offshore in countries like India due to the sheer manpower needed to find and secure links. If you use sites like Upwork to search for experienced link builders, make sure they use "white hat" tactics only, that is tactics that won't trigger Google's red flags.

Google's formula keeps changing—some links that used to be helpful can ultimately be either useless or detrimental to your link-building efforts. Even large companies are not immune. In 2011 an article in the *New York Times* detailed how J.C. Penney was penalized by Google for its link-building tactics.[8] This type of penalty could be disastrous for a company that relies heavily on organic inbound traffic from search engines. A website's traffic could plummet overnight due to a Google penalty. Besides illustrating the dangers in not diversifying your traffic sources, it also demonstrates the power of Google.

High-quality white-hat link building takes time and effort. It isn't easy, but succumbing to the lure of black-hat tactics can have serious repercussions. You may wish to consider using certain black-hat link building on websites that you don't mind "burning" through—that is, disposing of it if it does get penalized. But be sure to keep your most important websites free from any black-hat link building. The risk is just not worth the reward.

There are many useful resources for white-hat link building, including:

- Moz.com
- Backlinko.com
- Search Engine Journal
- EricWard.com

The topic of link building is as broad as PR. Books have been written about this one subject alone. One book that provides an excellent introduction and overview to the world of link building is written by Eric Ward, *Ultimate Guide to Link Building: How to Build Backlinks, Authority and Credibility for Your Website, and Increase Click Traffic and Search Ranking* (Entrepreneur Press, 2013).

---

[8] http://searchengineland.com/new-york-times-exposes-j-c-penney-link-scheme-that-causes-plummeting-rankings-in-google-64529

Here are some tips for getting started with link building:

1. Use free tools to check out your competitors. By looking at what links they have, you can figure out a way to also get those same links. Three of the most popular tools include Semrush.com, Ahrefs.com, and Moz.com. All have paid upgrade versions, but the free versions give you quite a bit of insight as well.
2. Use the same tools to review your own website. Compare how your link profile stacks up against your competitors.
3. Create a strategy and time line to go after the same types of links as your competitors, at a minimum. If they have a link to them from an article, this signals you may need a comprehensive PR strategy to get a similar link. If they have links from local or business directories, seek out the same.
4. Avoid going after black-hat links unless the website you're using it on is "disposable."
5. Keep up-to-date on the latest link-building opportunities from the sites listed above, and put it into practice.
6. Always be on the lookout for creative means to secure an inbound link. It could be getting a link in exchange for a testimonial you leave on a website. It could be contributing a donation and getting a link on the thank-you page. The possibilities are endless.

Sell Online

As mentioned previously, one possible long-term tactic that could help you stack the first page of Google with natural, positive results is to sell products online with your brand name in the title.

The ultimate goal is to have sites such as eBay, Amazon, and others rank high. If you went further and sold your products through distributors and other websites, you may even get a Google Shopping block to show up and dominate the top section of the search results.

But what if your business is a service or doesn't have a physical product to sell?

That's where e-books can come in. These days, anyone can write a book with little to no experience and self-publish it on Amazon's Kindle platform. Then a little work publicizing your book to related blogs (paid or unpaid), and you have book reviews helping your cause as well. Why not consider turning your e-book into a physical book? Self-publishing has never been simpler. Physical books are fabulous ways to promote yourself at trade shows and events.

How about getting even more creative? How about starting a product line for your brand? You've seen restaurants that sell their own gear. You could easily create coffee mugs, flash drives, T-shirts, hats, and more with your brand and offer those for sale online.

Take it one step further and create a separate e-commerce site just for selling your new branded products or e-book! Because of its relation to your brand, it is very possible to have it rank high on Google without much work.

The fastest way to sell something online is through a classified website. Craigslist is the largest and most well-known, but others include country-specific ones like Kijiji.ca in Canada.

Setting up your own e-commerce store can be done by using one of the following three major players: Amazon WebStore, Yahoo Stores, and eBay Stores. Each service has slightly different features that make it well-suited to certain types of sellers.

Yahoo Stores, originally launched in 1998, is one of the most complete e-commerce platforms for small businesses. Yahoo Stores start from $26 per month at the time of this writing, with fees of 1.5 percent or lower. Customers also have access to powerful e-commerce functionality such as real-time ordering and linking to inventory data.

Amazon's obvious advantage is the access to its huge customer base and the ability to participate in their popular Prime program, which offers free one- or two-day shipping.

eBay allows for auction format listings and branded stores.

When it comes to selling branded products, e-books, or information products to protect your online reputation, the only limit is your imagination!

Using Wikipedia to Build Online Reputation

There are certain sites that Google places high importance on. These are known as authoritative websites. Wikipedia is without a doubt one of them. Generally when you search for something, Wikipedia will be one of the top results that come up. It makes sense to want to have a Wikipedia page for the name you are trying to protect through online reputation management. If you have a Wikipedia page for your brand or company, it not only pushes all the other results down by one listing, but it also makes you look more authoritative and credible.

The biggest hurdle is that you can't just create any page on Wikipedia and expect it to stand. The online resource site has very strict guidelines on both what types of pages can be created and what content can be written on the page. Their editors are vigilant like hawks, watching for any changes to existing pages or new pages

RepGold Tip:

Through a lot of painful trial and error, the best recommendation I have for using Wikipedia is to hire an experienced Wikipedia writer to help guide you. Yes, you can attempt to do it yourself, but the time required to understand all their policies and the embarrassment you'll run into when things get deleted just aren't worth it.

being created. If there are any violations, they will delete the entries or entire pages without hesitation.

Wikipedia forbids its editors to be available for hire, but through some legwork you can still find many enterprising writers who have multiple editor accounts. The best places to seek them out are on freelance websites such as Upwork.com or Peopleperhour.com.

The number-one most important factor in whether or not a Wikipedia page is feasible is this: **Do you have credible, third-party mentions that you can use as sources?**

If you don't, you will not be able to create a Wikipedia page, with very few exceptions. Let's look at each part of that statement:

Credible: Wikipedia doesn't want people to simply make things up, for obvious reasons. They want their site to be neutral, authoritative, and true. To do this, they rightly assume that if you, your company, or your product has been mentioned on a credible website, you are also credible. For example, if there is an article in the *New York Times* that mentions you, that is highly credible. It doesn't have to be on the national level of the *Times*. Even mentions in more niche, industry websites can be used as sources. But generally, "credible" means a news website of some kind. It can also mean academic books or journals. Personal blogs don't really count unless it's a pretty highly touted blogger.

Wikipedia has recently tightened up their requirements even further. For instance, a reprint of a press release on a news site isn't considered credible. They have moved to only allowing articles that are originally written by a reporter/blogger as a source.

Third party: Simply using your own website as a source won't cut it, again for obvious reasons. Anyone can write anything they want about themselves on their own website, and therefore you cannot use that as a source for Wikipedia. It must be another party that has nothing to do with you.

Here we see once again the power and the importance of public relations for your online reputation management efforts. Not only does PR help you immensely with positive search results, but it can help with link building and Wikipedia page creation.

If you are in a situation where you do not have any credible, third-party mentions, consider creating a PR strategy pronto or contact an agency like Firecracker PR.

Corporate Website Site Links

The name of the game in online reputation management is effective control of Google's first page of search results. Always keep that goal in mind. Similar to how the end zone is the goal in football, all your efforts should contribute toward moving the ball to achieve that goal. This means that you constantly need to be learning and staying up-to-date on how Google works and what changes they've implemented. Knowing what Google likes is half the battle.

One example of this is site links. You've likely seen them before. Site links are simply links to other areas of a website and are displayed under the main search result.

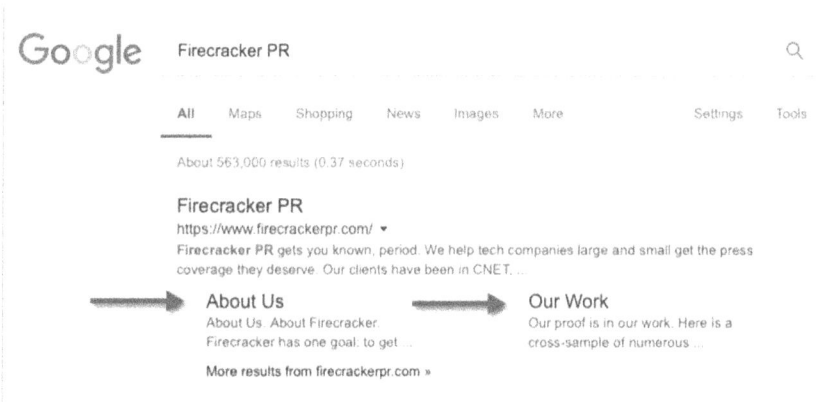

From a user perspective, this reduces the number of clicks they need to make. Rather than clicking to a company's home page, then clicking a link on the main menu bar, they simply click on a site link and go straight there. It reduces the number of clicks a user has to make by taking them directly to sub–web pages with a site, bypassing the home page completely.

Can you see why site links are so valuable from an ORM perspective? It's all about real estate that the owner controls … search-engine-results real estate.

The stack of three site links, with two blocks in each row, results in taking up about eleven lines of space. This effectively pushes all other search results lower. It is a proven fact that users always click on links "above the fold" (the part of a web page you see without having to scroll down) more than "below the fold" (the part of a web page you need to scroll down to view). A study in 2014 by Moz.com found that the first search result got a whopping 31.24 percent of all clicks. From there it trails off to only 3.73 percent for positions six through ten, which typically is below the fold. With a careful plan, you can create a monopoly of search-engine-results space that you control.

To make matters worse, Google keeps changing how they serve up search results. Google AdWords advertising used to be shown on both the top and right-hand side of the search results pages. As I'm writing this book, Google has already transitioned to just showing ads at the top, as well as snippets and answers to questions. The net result is that organic search results are fewer and fewer on page 1.

As with most things to do with Google organic search results, there's nothing you can do that directly creates these site links. Instead, what you want and need to do is to position your website in the best possible light so that Google is able to show your site links.

Without going into too many granular details, this means that the links on your main menu bar from your home page need to be in a format that Google can see and understand. If your website is coded in Flash or mostly using images or Java, this will make it difficult to achieve site links. Instead, keep the menu bar simple. Make them simple text links to the subpages.

Also remember to create unique Title and Description tags for each of those subpages that come from the main menu links.

If this is starting to get too technical, don't worry. Find anyone who knows even the most basic web design and they will understand what this means. Having unique tags shows Google that these pages are different and important.

Finally, site links are likely driven by your website visitors clicking on these menu links. As a rule of thumb, also repeat the main menu links that are on the top of your website in the footer section way at the bottom of your site. Keep it in simple, small font.

One important tip that relates to SEO in general but may also apply for achieving site links is to ensure you have a "sitemap" for your website. A sitemap is just a page or file that tells your website visitors or search engines what all the pages on your site are. Most search engines can crawl and index your website without a sitemap, but if your website is large or complicated, it can hinder that process.

An "XML sitemap" is a simple file you can generate and upload into Google Webmaster Tools that tells search engines all the pages on your site they should know about. Ask your SEO contractor or web designer for help here. Also ask them to create an actual page that is a sitemap. This is just a simple web page that lists the most important subpages on a site.

Firecracker

Contact Us

About Us   Public Relations   SEO Marketing   Content Marketing   Our Work   Blog   Contact Us   Sitemap

SITEMAP

Pages
- About Us
- Apply
- Blog
- Contact Us
- Content Marketing
- Front Page
- Industry
- Our Work
- Public Relations
- Questionnaire
- Sample Page
- SEO Marketing
- Sitemap
- THANK YOU

Posts by category
- Category: Blog
  - The 1 Key to Successful PR (Part 2)
  - The 1 Key to Successful PR
  - The 1 Key to Successful Content Marketing
  - 6 Secrets to More PR in Less Than an Hour a Day
  - 104 Ideas for Press Releases Infographic
  - SEO and PR Strategy Using Awards
  - Why We Should Thank Marissa Mayer and Yahoo
  - Animal Planet Shows Us How to Destroy Your Reputation
  - The Art of the Exclusive
  - How Product Marketing Can Help Every Company
  - Comparison of Wire Services for Press Release Distribution
  - 6 Steps to Building Trust Online (So Google and Prospects Love You)

By doing all these best practice tactics, you position yourself for the best possible chance to get Google to show site links. When it comes to search engines, nothing is guaranteed. But a 75 percent chance is always better than a 15 percent chance.

THE LAST STRAW: WHEN EVERYTHING ELSE FAILS ... LAWSUITS AND LEGAL OPTIONS

Disclaimer: I am not an attorney, and the following information is not to be considered legal advice. Before doing anything that involves the law, always consult an experienced attorney in your particular field.

I've chosen to put this section toward the end of this chapter because the first instinct of most people when trying to defend against online slander is to see red and want to sue, sue, sue. But lawsuits aren't something to be taken lightly. The cost—both financial and emotional—of an actual lawsuit that ends up going all the way to trial could be enormous. Seriously weigh the cost and benefit. Lawsuits have been known to end both businesses and marriages.

If that wasn't enough, the actual prospect of using legal action successfully to combat negative online reputation is not that great. There's a relatively unknown law in America called the "Communications Decency Act" where Section 47 U.S.C. § 230(c)[9] allows websites such as Pissed Consumer and Ripoff Report exclusion from certain types of civil liability that seeks to treat the website owner as the publisher or speaker of user-generated content. This means that even if users post things that are lies or falsehoods, the website owner is not legally liable.

This hasn't stopped people from trying, though. Sites like Ripoff Report are widely hated by business owners. For as much as they provide a genuine outlet for customers to air grievances, there are

---

[9] https://en.wikipedia.org/wiki/Section_230_of_the_Communications_Decency_Act

many business owners who claim that the complaints are either false or misleading. To add fuel to the fire, Ripoff Report has a "Corporate Advocacy, Business Remediation & Customer Satisfaction Program" that can charge anywhere from thousands to tens of thousands of dollars to supposedly help companies deal with the complaints. Ripoff Report has a policy of never removing content that's been posted on their site, which leads some to question the efficacy and value of this program.

Other sites like Pissed Consumer do not take quite such a hard line on potential removal of user-posted content. According to their FAQs: "Does Pissed Consumer remove reviews from its website? Yes. Pissed Consumer removes reviews from its website if it receives an order from a Court or a notarized letter from the person who posted it."

Getting an order from the court is not necessarily an easy task. There are certain attorneys who specialize in internet defamation that should be consulted. One notable attorney is Mr. Ken Hutcherson of Hutcherson Law in Dallas, Texas.

Hutcherson posted an article on February 24, 2011, on SearchEngineLand.com that gave some hope to beleaguered companies hurt by Ripoff Report that there was another way. Even though Ripoff Report never deleted postings from their site, if there was a way to have Google just not show certain pages from Ripoff Report, that would be almost as good. Mr. Hutcherson's article outlined the following steps:

First, file a lawsuit against the original author of the report for defamation, business disparagement, false light, or any other claim that is legally appropriate. The big point here is that you have to prove your case in a court of law—you have the burden to prove the report made about you is false.

Be honest with yourself (otherwise, you're just wasting time and money). If the report about you is true (or if you can't prove your case), you do not have a valid claim for defamation, and this option will not work for you. Again, the key here is being able to prove your case in a court of law. If you can't do that, game over. You're stuck with one of the other options above.

Also, you should only sue the author of the report—do not sue Google. Your lawsuit will cost a fortune (Google has plenty of good lawyers), fail very quickly, and you will only serve to anger the one company that can help you the most.

Second, obtain a court order declaring the offending report to be false and defamatory (this of course assumes you win your case). The specific content of this order can take various forms, but you should make sure to seek an order that refers to the offending report specifically.

Third, present the court order to Google.

Remember, do not sue Google! Your goal is to get Google to be on your side and delist the content from their search engine, not to get into a legal fight with a company that has more lawyers than most small countries.

When the court order is ready, submit the court order through Google's official submission process. Their link for this changes, so just Google "Removing Content from Google," and one of the top results should be a form with steps to walk you through it.

At this point you may have your doubts. Could little ol' you really get big ol' Google to not show a certain web page on their search results? The answer is unequivocally *yes*. I know because I have personally used this tactic with success. The tactic doesn't just work for Ripoff Report, it works for any type of website that has false content, be it Ripoff Report or a personal blog site.

One firsthand example is a project we worked on for a prominent businessman who was being slandered on a personal blog site that ranked extraordinarily well on Google because the site had a ton of content. We secured a court order, submitted it to Google, answered a few follow-up questions, and had the site delisted from Google's search results.

RepGold Tip:

Remember, in order to get a court order in the first place, you are going to have to legally prove that the claims against you are false. Being able to meet a legal burden of proof is far different than just "he said, she said." So first make sure you are really in the right, then make sure you will be able to prove it.

And again, when it comes to legal matters, don't just take my advice but rather seek out experienced legal counsel for your particular needs.

6
IMMUNIZING THROUGH SUPERIOR CUSTOMER SERVICE

When it comes to preventing negative search results from showing up on the first page of Google, the best bet is to immunize yourself so you don't face the predicament in the first place. There are two main options that work best to prevent negative listings: superior customer service and consistent public relations.

Entire brands can be built on better customer service: Southwest Airlines, Costco, Nordstrom, Zappos.com, Apple Genius Bars. These brands are more or less known for their excellence at taking care of their customers. What does that really mean? It creates a strong brand identity that attracts new customers while building loyalty that keeps existing ones…a powerful one-two combo. Think of stories you have read in the press about companies going above and beyond the call of duty to help a customer in need.

Ironically, and sadly, many companies think they are better at service than they actually are. It is easy to type "excellent customer service" into corporate executive plans.

RepGold Tip:

Many of the long-term tactics discussed earlier to repair reputation can also be used to immunize your reputation. For those who skimmed through that section, make sure to take the time and go through my suggestions. Each of those tactics listed in previous chapters has been tested in real-world situations and has been found to provide value.

Unfortunately, those same companies aren't as good at service as they think they are.

Here are some tactics you can implement to create a brand with superior service that can weather any storm.

THE GOLDEN RULE

Do unto others as you would have them do unto you.
— Matthew 7:12

Those immortal words from the Bible still ring true today. It is generally called "the Golden Rule," and it is a principle that has amazingly been found throughout various cultures and peoples.

When it comes to excelling in customer service, the Golden Rule rules. Treat your customers as you would wish to be treated. Put yourself in their shoes:

- Would you really want to be stuffed into what airlines call seats these days, with grumpy flight attendants and everything a paid upgrade?
- Would you really want to be put on hold for 25 minutes listening to soft pop hits of the 1980s, only to speak with a customer service rep with a poorly masked foreign accent?
- Would you really want to be subjected to hardball negotiations with a car dealer salesperson who has to constantly go ask his manager for every little concession?

The Golden Rule is one of the easiest concepts in the world to understand intuitively, yet strangely it is one of the hardest concepts to implement in business.

In my opinion, the best remedy for bad customer service is a free market. The more competition, the more likely a business who takes the best care of their clients will survive. The more monopolistic or closed the market, the less a business will care. After all, what choice do they have?

Even better are online review sites like Yelp or TripAdvisor that allow just about anyone to leave a review of their experience. Companies are nervous that they don't create a bad experience that leads to the dreaded one-star review, and rightly so. Now the power is firmly back in the court of consumers. Whether we like it or not, consumers have many more outlets to hold businesses accountable, and this power (like any) can be abused.

As an example, there was an article published in the *New York Times* about the disastrous movie box office for the summer of 2017 that had many producers pointing a guilty finger at the review site Rotten Tomatoes.[10]

Want to find the chinks in your service armor? Go undercover as

---

[10] https://www.nytimes.com/2017/09/07/business/media/rotten-tomatoes-box-office.html?mcubz=0&_r=0

a customer in your own business and see firsthand. Contact customer service with a problem. Go through the hoops. Then ask yourself, is this how I'd want to be treated?

Listen ... Really Listen

> *Most people do not listen with the intent to understand; they listen with the intent to reply.*
>
> **—Stephen R. Covey**

The art of listening is fast becoming extinct. Covey's phrase better sums up the current culture than any other time. Yet when you come across people who truly do listen, you notice them, and you appreciate them. How many times have you asked someone how they are but didn't really take the time to truly find out how they were doing?

Nothing infuriates people more than when they feel like a helpless cog in a massive machine. Take for example your experience dealing with the DMV or any other government bureaucracy. When you come to any such department with a problem, do you feel like they are really listening? Most feel their concerns are dismissed, because frankly there is no downside for the large organization to ignoring complaints.

Now contrast that with companies that provide excellent service. With few exceptions, one of their traits is they are good listeners. When it comes to customer service, your employees simply can't excel at resolving problems unless they can listen both intently and empathetically.

Through listening instead of rushing to speak, you can determine:

a) Is this customer just venting?
b) What sort of resolution does this customer want?

More often than not, simply letting the customer know that you've

heard them and you sympathize with them will go a long way toward
defusing a potentially bad situation. This can be done by being quiet
while the customer talks, asking probing questions to get more information, and making statements that show you sympathize with them.

Example: "I can completely understand how you'd be angry. I'd
be angry too if I were in your shoes."

Making statements that reflect what the customer just told you is
another way to show them that you're listening:

Example: "So just to make sure I understand you correctly, you
are upset because your ticket wasn't properly refunded."

The risk of a customer feeling as if their concerns aren't being
listened to is that they will go onto the internet and vent on websites
that could directly harm your reputation. Much better to quickly resolve the issue before it festers. Training your customer service team
to become good listeners can build and maintain ORM, and being a
good listener can go a long way toward awesome customer service.

Under-Promise and Over-Deliver (UPOD)

Promises are like crying babies in a theater,
they should be carried out at once.
—Norman Vincent Peale

One way to consistently delight customers is to under-promise and
over-deliver, or as I refer to it, UPOD.

UPOD's exact opposite is OPUD: over-promising and under-de-
livering. You never want to OPUD.

OPUDing is a sure way to send disgruntled people to the internet
to complain. It sounds simplistic, but in fact the differences in outcome can be dramatic. The long-term effects of encouraging UPOD
can have huge positive benefits, whereas the opposite will drive disgruntled consumers online to lodge complaints that will only cause
more headaches and damage.

Under-promising and over-delivering can also be thought of as managing expectations. By raising expectations too high, you set a very tough bar to clear. Inevitably, the rash of promises can't be kept.

This is a tempting path for salespeople to take, especially in industries or companies that traditionally employ aggressive sales tactics. This includes timeshares, telemarketing, or car salespeople. Basically any industry that has a bad rap for poor sales experiences has one for a reason.

One remedy to reconciling aggressive sales goals with customer satisfaction is not just compensating based on closed deals but also on the number of retained customers or high scores on satisfaction surveys.

UPODing not only applies to the sales staff but also to the customer support system. When faced with complicated service issues, it is best not to make promises that cannot be kept. Instead, do some fact-finding to ensure the resolution can be made. For instance, if a customer's product is broken, do not promise her or him you can replace it with a new product unless you are absolutely sure you can. And make sure when you say "new" that it isn't actually refurbished.

There are two paths to take when UPODing:

One is to "delight" the customer. Think of the online shoe company Zappos or the hotel chain Ritz-Carlton and their stories of legendary service that have become mythical.

Two is to "facilitate" the customer by making the sales and service process as effortless as possible. On the sales side, this might mean shorter sales engagements with far less pressure and more transparency upfront. Arm your sales team with more information during pre-sales to qualify leads. On the support side, this might mean offering as many channels of support as possible (email, live phone, live chat on website, forum/message board).

Either way, practicing UPOD while avoiding OPUD can play a huge role in happy customers and fewer negative experiences.

Follow-Through

> *Those people blessed with the most talent don't necessarily outperform everyone else. It's the people with follow-through who excel.*
>
> **—Mary Kay Ash**

Believe it or not, procrastination can not only occur in someone's personal life, it can also crop up within a company's sales and support staff. Procrastination can take the form of forgetfulness, laziness, or fear. The result is the same: *lack of follow-through*. The consequence? Angry customers who are ready and willing to tell everyone how your business doesn't keep their word. The thought of this should strike fear into the hearts of both small- and large-business owners.

One way to ensure that tasks are followed through to completion when it comes to dealing with prospects or customers is the judicious use of a Customer Relationship Management system. It can be a software platform as complex as Salesforce, or it can be as basic as using the free Google Sheets spreadsheet among employees to track engagements.

The basic goal is to hold employees whose job requires them to engage on a regular basis with consumers responsible. Software or processes like CRM allow the user to record what was promised, the date it was promised, and the target date to deliver on the promise. If that promise cannot be kept, there has to be a legitimate reason why; the customer should be notified as soon as possible as to the delay of the resolution. Do not keep the customer in the dark. Ongoing communication is key to customers having a sense that they are cared for and taken seriously.

The best system in the world can't replace proactive employees who take to heart the goal of providing exceptional service. Conversely, lackadaisical employees can be serious deadweight to an organization, and one bad employee can negatively impact dozens or hundreds of customers. The resulting damage to the company's online reputation can happen almost instantly and require hours of painstaking online repair work as I've outlined in this book. Worse yet, it will certainly impact sales in a bad way.

Therefore, superior customer service starts with your HR department, and if you own and operate a very small business, that HR department is most likely just you.

CUSTOMER SERVICE JUDO AND COUNTERINTUITIVE LOGIC

A soft answer turns away wrath, but a harsh word stirs up anger.
—Proverbs 15:1

Judo is a Japanese martial art that has a core element where "softness controls hardness." The philosophy means that directly resisting a more powerful opponent will result in your defeat, whereas adjusting to and evading your opponent's attack will cause him to be defeated.[11] In a similar vein, customer service should be approached like judo. Instead of directly responding to a customer's harsh words with your own blunt answers, find ways to redirect and evade their attacks.

Here are some practical examples.

In the event that a customer has had a poor experience, don't seek to nitpick at his or her story in order to try to find a "gotcha." You may win the argument on a technicality, but if the customer's anger isn't resolved, you lose the war in the long run. An "experience" is just that: a subjective feeling that the customer holds to be true. Logic cannot overcome it. Instead, use customer service judo and bypass the anger of the experience. A more counterintuitive and ORM-friendly solution would be to redirect the angry consumer and ask what he/she would like to see done in order to remedy the

---

[11] On the Origins of Sports: The Early History and Original Rules of Everybody's Favorite Games. Gary Belsky & Neil Fine. 2016.

situation, thus making the customer happy.

Customers are so used to being told what will happen that this redirection may catch them off-guard. With just a couple of sentences, suddenly their anger and sense of loss of control has been flipped around to where control is firmly back in their hands.

Don't minimize the power of the sense of control. There is a well-known phenomenon in psychology called "learned helplessness." As an example, a person (or animal) gives up trying to avoid pain because they've learned that there is no control over it. The psychological impact is immense. The person experiences anger, depression, and stress, plus they have difficulty solving problems.

Does this sound like a potential angry customer who believes they have been wronged? By using customer service judo and asking the angry consumer what they would like to see happen to fix the situation, the control is essentially given back to them. The result is that shift in tone or tactics neutralizes the learned helplessness.

Customer service judo works for any product- or service-based business.

Let's take the example of an agency or consulting firm that is dealing with a disgruntled client. The client feels that the monthly retainers they have paid have not been worth it. You can certainly make the case that they got A, B, and C for their retainer

RepGold Tip:

Why not give out colored belts, like in judo, to customer service reps who demonstrate the ability to redirect bad-service cases into positive resolutions? Imagine having black belt service reps! (Not to be confused with other disciplines such as Six Sigma, which also uses belt designations.)

fee. But again, that logic may not tamp down their anger.

Using customer service judo, ask the client what you as an agency could do to make them feel satisfied. Offer them a choice to continue doing work for another month for free to help achieve further results. Even if those results don't materialize, just the offer may greatly diminish their anger.

Customer service judo takes practice. It's not in our nature. Human nature is to repay evil with evil, and an eye for an eye. We instinctively want to lash out when being attacked. Customer service reps are no different. They are human and on the front lines, taking a beating every day. As a small business or large company, pay attention and assist the customer support team. Empower them to resolve situations in a positive manner. Make sure they feel appreciated. Train them in how to do customer service judo. They in turn will help defuse problems that could lead to negative reputation down the road.

Turn Complainers into Fans

One of the biggest contradictions in business is that almost every company understands the importance of good customer service, but few are able to deliver it consistently. Whether it's a matter of poor hiring or poor training, the outcome is the same: unhappy customers. As this book has noted multiple times, complainers can have their unhappiness magnified and spread across the internet, damaging the hard-earned reputation of your business.

Through tactics like customer service judo, there does exist a real opportunity to convert the complainers into fans. It sounds ludicrous but consider that the passion that leads customers to take the time and effort to go online and type up their complaints reflects the passion that they had when they bought from you. After all, love and hate are two sides of the same coin. Both are driven by extreme emotions.

That passion hasn't gone away. Rather, their disappointment in suffering from bad service has channeled the passion from excitement to fury. Your job is to reverse that passion back to excitement. It is possible, more possible than most companies believe. The strategy is to utilize the tips in this section of the book, then compensate the customer in a way that will shock them into becoming a fan, in a pleasant way.

Don't Forget the Top of the Funnel

Customer service generally deals with post-sales support. But another form of service is at the very top of a funnel: right at the point of a prospect trying to contact sales. Quality leads are the lifeblood for any company. Yet it's amazing how poorly most organizations do responding in a timely fashion to inquiries. How many times have you asked a question by filling out a form or sending to a generic "sales@" email address, only for it to go into a black hole? Or only to get a response weeks later?

A 2017 study by Drift found that more than half (55 percent) of companies did not even respond to inquiries over the course of five business days.[12] Needless to say, those that don't respond quickly aren't going to engender warm, fuzzy feelings. Not only will they likely miss out on the sale, they will likely ding their reputation in the eye of the prospect.

This sort of harm to a company's reputation can be detrimental precisely because it is so hidden. It's not broadcast on a review website to see and be exposed. *It's in the thoughts of the potential sale or consumer, which then may spread in the form of bad word of mouth to their particular industry.* Many business industries can be quite small in the sense that everyone knows everyone. Poor word of mouth about a pre-sales or sales inquiry can deter others from considering your company in the future.

---

[12] https://blog.drift.com/lead-response-survey/

7
MONITORING ONLINE REPUTATION

THE IMPORTANCE OF MONITORING

Without a way to regularly monitor your current status on search engines, it is next to impossible to decide how effective your efforts are. Since Google is constantly making tweaks to their search algorithm, their results will fluctuate. Periodically Google will roll out massive new changes that they codename, such as "Penguin" or "Panda." These changes will set the SEO world afire with conjecture and analysis. The best advice is for you, your marketing team, or your customer service team to stay up-to-date with the latest information.

Manual Checking

The most obvious way to check search engine rankings is to simply type the brand name in question into Google and review the generated results.

One important note is to use a web browser that you normally don't use every day. The reason for this is that Google is starting to customize search results based on how often you visited a site based on the search results they generated. Thus, what you see may be a distorted version of what are the actual neutral results. Therefore, if you use Google Chrome as your everyday browser, use alternate browsers such as Microsoft Edge, Firefox, Safari, or Opera to manually check search results.

RepGold Tip:
One of the best sources of information on the latest search engine tactics is Moz.com. Make sure to sign up for their newsletters with the top industry changes and tips you need to be aware of. The lines between SEO and other areas such as content generation, design, and user interactivity are blurring considerably. The more informed you are, the more effective your online reputation management efforts will be.

Google Alerts

Google Alerts is still one of the most powerful tools out there for monitoring reputation and public relations efforts. And keeping in line with Google's philosophy, it is absolutely free to use. With Google Alerts, you can have notifications sent to you whenever anything on the internet is new with your name in it.

To start, go to http://www.google.com/alerts and walk through the step-by-step process. For online reputation management purposes, select "All Results." Thus, if anyone posts anything negative on a website or message board/forum, you will be alerted and have a chance to take action.

Social Media Monitoring

The gold standard at the time of this writing for monitoring your brand across all major social media platforms is Hootsuite (www.hootsuite.com). Starting from $29 a month, you get a powerful tool that does the hard work for you where Google Alerts cannot reach. It's well worth the small monthly payment in this day and age when problems that crop up on social media can spread like wildfire around the world in a matter of hours. Online tools come and go. Google "social media monitoring" to see what other options there are beyond Hootsuite.

RepGold

Our sister business RepGold takes a unique approach to monitoring your reputation by assigning you an Online Reputation Score (ORS). Using a similar approach that credit scores use for individual persons, your ORS for your business or individual name gives you a quick snapshot in time of how your online reputation is doing. It takes into account all the major search engines and uses a complex formula to produce one score that provides a lot of information in one number.

Learn more about RepGold at www.repgold.com.

8
PUBLIC RELATIONS

Public relations can be a powerful ally in your quest to create bullet-proof Total Online Reputation. That's because PR is meant to try to harness the power of the press in your favor. Like it or not, even with the recent issues with "fake news," reading about a company in an article is still considered to be more trustworthy than an advertisement.

The field of PR is massive and beyond the scope of this book. But here are some important tips on why and how PR can be used effectively to create a reputation of gold.

TOP SIX REASONS WHY PR IS KING

1. **PR is cheaper than advertising.**
   Think about magazine ads in either widely distributed magazines or more industry-specific magazines. Either way, you're looking at about $6,000 for a full-page print ad. And

that's not including the creative, graphic design, and time spent for multiple approvals. When it's done, you have an advertisement that even if you hit the right timing in the marketplace, only 10 percent of viewers will look at and even fewer will remember.

Since advertising proponents constantly tout the need for repeated advertising frequency, you're looking at close to $50,000 for an extended ad campaign with few tangible results except awareness. That same $50,000 could get you at least one year's worth of PR services, and with a properly crafted strategy, could positively impact your sales multiple times over. For a great look at the end of advertising, read *The Fall of Advertising & the Rise of PR* by Al Ries and Laura Ries (HarperBusiness, 2004).

2. **If you hit it big, you can hit it *big*.**
   Coming up with a strategic PR plan requires a little bit of good luck, timing, and a lot of pitches to the press, which can result in a huge payday. The power of the press and an innovative campaign that strikes a chord with your target audience can do wonders for sales, far greater than any ad campaign, unless you have the millions of dollars it would take to run a far-reaching advertising run.

   Mike Lindell, founder of MyPillow, says it was one particular PR break that jump-started his company. An interview with Mike in the Minneapolis *Star Tribune* that ran in their business section in January of 2011 drove so much traffic that their website went "crazy." According to a Bloomberg profile on MyPillow, "in a single day the company made more sales than it had in the previous six months. The surge lasted three months."[13] Now that's called hitting it *big*. Could you come up with an interesting story that your local newspaper would

---

[13] "The Preposterous Success Story of America's Pillow King," Bloomberg.com, Josh Dean, January 11, 2017.

write about?

3. **PR has credibility, advertising has no credibility.**

    The reason why PR is so much more powerful than advertising boils down to credibility. When we view ads, we know we are being sold to. When a newscaster or reporter talks or writes about a company, we think the report is an impartial third party of information. Therefore, we take what they have to say much more seriously. That is why public relations is often referred to as "earned media" while advertising is referred to as "paid media." They are two sides of the same coin: media. But in the case of PR, you cannot buy yourself press coverage. If a reporter is going to write about you, it's because you earned that story by pitching them and convincing them your story was newsworthy. Conversely, all advertising (paid media) requires is money. Earned media's credibility amplifies your message and builds awareness with your target audience.

4. **We are bombarded with advertising.**

    In relation to my point above, the average person is bombarded with advertisements more than ever now. Studies vary, with numbers in the thousands of ads that we are exposed to. TV shows are interrupted by them every twelve minutes. Ads pop up on the internet. Inboxes are flooded with spam. Telemarketers hunt us down on our home or mobile phones. Now do you believe that ads are not credible? The fact of the matter is, if it's an ad, we've trained ourselves to tune it out. And even the odd catchy ad that does manage to make us chuckle doesn't do enough to actually make us use or buy the product. I think of Matthew McConaughey and his endorsement of Lincoln cars through a series of television ads. I'm a big fan of McConaughey, and as much as I thought the television ads were compelling, when it came time for me to buy a car, I passed on a Lincoln. Did the ad do its job? Yes, in the sense that I remember the ads. But it did not convert me into a customer. And in that regard, the ad failed.

5. **PR is highly creative.**

Let's face it, we have been bombarded with advertising in North America since the invention of TV. When we view an ad on TV, in a magazine, or online, we are alert that someone is trying to sell us something (although the clever attempts using "native advertising" can be pretty fuzzy).

PR is a completely different ball game, and the sky's the limit. Your creativity is the only constraint on what type of PR and how much press coverage you can get. One master of PR is the legendary founder of Virgin, Sir Richard Branson. The seed of his outrageous publicity events was planted with his founding of Virgin Atlantic. Somehow, he needed a way to compete with British Airways, which had a multimillion-dollar advertising budget. Branson dressed up as the airline captain and got front-page coverage. That's about as tame as his stunts got. A quick search of Google comes up with many articles that list the numerous PR and marketing stunts he's done over his life. Whether it's driving a tank in Times Square, dressing as a bride, or jumping off the top of a casino, you can be sure that every event Branson pulled off led to press coverage that drove massive attention to his brand.

Branson's insatiable desire to get coverage by performing so many clever PR stunts created an entire subset of articles written about the initial article. That is great PR. Now, I am not asking business execs to suit up in mascot outfits and hit the neighborhood, but look at your own talents and, yes, inhibitions, and come up with a way to get PR. It is up to your creativity and, really, the sky is the limit.

6. **PR can build powerful brands.**

The number-one misconception is that advertising builds brands. Nothing could be further from the truth. PR builds brands, and advertising maintains them. This is the central thesis in the book *The Fall of Advertising & the Rise of PR* by Al Ries and Laura Ries. As the book promotion says, "Today's major brands are born with publicity, not advertising. A closer look at the history of the most successful modern brands shows this to be true. In fact, an astonishing number of brands, including Palm, Starbucks, the Body Shop, Wal-Mart, Red Bull and Zara, have been built with virtually no advertising." I'd add to that Elon Musk and his flagship companies of Tesla and SpaceX. Both have disrupted their respective industries, and both have been breathlessly reported on by the media. Like Sir Richard Branson, Elon Musk is a master of publicity. To grow your brand, you need PR. To maintain your brand, you need advertising. And that's a good thing. It means that any start-up can ignore the misconception of requiring a multimillion-dollar ad budget. With some creativity and effort, any new brand can get press coverage. Start small, think locally, and with your resources on hand, come up with an authentic and fun PR plan.

Maria and Peter knew right from the start that in order to compete with the big guys, they'd need to think creatively. They came up with a contest targeting local high school students in disadvantaged neighborhoods. Playing up on their "Dreamy Cupcakes" name, they called it "I Have a Dream Contest" to evoke memories of the great Reverend Martin Luther King, Jr. The contest was simple: students were to come up with their dream of one good thing they could do for their neighborhood that could help it for the better.

Peter reached out to local television and NEWSPAPERS, who ate the idea up. Students were to do a selfie video of a short speech on what their dream was for the neighborhood and why it was important to them. The winner was allocated $10,000 to carry out that dream. This simple contest not only raised a ton of press coverage for Dreamy Cupcakes, it was a fun way for Maria and Peter to give back to the community.

The Most Important PR Tip You'll Ever Read

Through all my years of dealing with editors and reporters, I've come to the conclusion that if you do not follow this tip, most of your PR efforts will be futile.

So here it is. If you want to be successful in PR, **you need to think like the press does.**

That's it?

Yup. But trust me, it is easier said than done. That's because we all suffer from "me-itis."

This is a syndrome where we love to drone on and on about how great our companies are, how wonderful our new products are, and how important our mission statement is. The truth of the matter is, no one really cares, least of all the press. After all, why should they? Their job isn't advertising, it's news. And in news, they have to find stories that are newsworthy. Are you paying attention?

That is the secret right there. *Newsworthy.*

Every time you contact an editor or reporter, ask yourself, "is this newsworthy?" If I were an editor or reporter, would I care? How can this be positioned so it is of interest to the readers of a newspaper, magazine, website, or blog? Again, this sounds easy, but in reality it is much harder than it seems.

It requires a fundamental shift in how you think. A shift away from "me, me, me" toward "you, you, you."

Next time you begin any PR efforts, remember: always think from the press's point of view and ask yourself, "how is this newsworthy?" You'll find this one tip alone will help you secure much more coverage.

The One Key to Successful PR

PR isn't easy. In fact, out of all the different marketing tactics out there, PR could be one of the most difficult. Not difficult like engineering or rocket science is difficult. But difficult in the sense that achieving media coverage consistently isn't easy.

Throughout the history of man, storytelling has been a tried-and-true way of communication. Before there were written records, history was transmitted through stories. Even today, we humans are born with an innate desire for stories. It's why kids delight in parents telling them stories, whether made up or from a book. It's why we go to movies or binge-watch Netflix series. We all want a good story.

And *storytelling* is the single-most important ingredient for success in PR.

Why? Well if you think about it, the answer is ob-

RepGold Tip:
Here is the single-most important secret to being more successful in PR. It's a secret that PR pros sometimes forget, but it's not one that reporters forget. Just remembering and focusing on this one secret could transform your PR efforts overnight.

vious. The goal of PR is to get the media to write about you. And the goal of media is to get people to read, listen, or watch. Going back full circle to our desire for stories, logically it makes sense that in order for you to successfully pitch to a reporter, you have to convince them that your story is one their readers will care about.

Therefore, you have to tell a compelling story to the reporter so they can be convinced that if they write about you, people will care. While the secret of storytelling seems obvious and easy, the devil is in the details. You might be dismayed and think that neither you nor your business has a story to tell.

Everyone has a story to tell … you just might not be fully aware of what it is.

That's where a good PR agency can come in and help. Here's an example of how any company can come up with a compelling story. One of my clients at Firecracker PR made valves for the oil and gas industry. On the surface, that sounds as if there's no real story there. But upon further inquiries, we discovered three storylines:

1. With some probing questions and research, I discovered that the inventor of this valve had a wonderful story on how and why he invented this new type of valve.
2. The valve was a unique design that fundamentally changed how oil and gas companies needed to service compressors, leading to huge safety benefits such as reduced workplace injuries.
3. Because the valve didn't require servicing as often, it also reduced methane emissions.

The first story angle was interesting enough to pique the interest of an editor at a large national magazine. The second storyline led to widespread coverage in industry magazines. The third storyline helped them win a major prestigious award in the category of green innovation. What looked like a simple valve in reality turned into three stories that helped boost PR efforts far beyond what the usual press release could ever hope to achieve.

Storytelling is powerful because at our core, all of us want to be told a story. Humans are hardwired to listen to well-told stories. The most gifted writers and speakers are those who know how to spin a good story. Truth be told, any business or person has a story inside them.

Here are the steps for you to discover and then unleash your inner story:

1. Identify your ideal client profile.
2. Figure out what keeps them up at night.
3. Choose an avatar.
4. Be persistent and consistent.

Ideal Client Profile

First of all, the key to a compelling story is to figure out your ideal client profile. Who are they? Is it a small-business owner or the CEO of a midsize company? Are they lower income or higher income? What are their hobbies? Where do they congregate online? Do they tend to be more conservative or liberal? Figuring out an ICP is actually critical to all sales, marketing, and branding efforts. If you don't really understand who your best customer is, take a look at your existing customers. What traits do they share? Spending time on honing your ICP will go a long way toward helping you craft your story.

Figure Out What Keeps Them Up at Night

Do they worry about their sales? Do they worry about hackers breaking into their network? Do they want a better way to monitor their health? Do they want to get rid of their acne? Do they want to keep their kids healthier? What is their pain point that your company helps solve?

Choose an Avatar

In Russell Brunson's book *Dotcom Secrets* (Morgan James Publishing, 2015), he refers to it as an "identity of an attractive character." I call it an avatar, but they both mean the same thing. Here are some identities Brunson outlines from which you can choose that naturally fit your company or yourself the best:

The Leader: "The identity of the leader is usually assumed by people whose goal is to lead their audiences from one place to another." You can be a leader either through fact (market leader) or through position (we are a leader in a specific type of manufacturing for instance).

The Adventurer or Crusader: "The adventurer is usually someone who is very curious, but he doesn't always have all of the answers. So he sets out on a journey to discover the ultimate truth." Think a mix of Richard Branson and Elon Musk. Or Porter Stansberry in the investment world. Or James Altucher.

The Reporter or Evangelist: "This identity is one that people use when they have not yet blazed a trail to share with an audience, but have a desire to." If you have a new means to good health, or your software secures networks particularly strongly, for instance. In both cases you have to educate the market by both asking questions and evangelizing.

The Reluctant Hero: "This is the humble hero who doesn't really want the spotlight or any fuss made over his discoveries. But he knows the information or secrets he has are so important that he must overcome his shyness and share them with the world." For those who are uncomfortable in the spotlight naturally, this is the role that may fit you the best by default.

These four avatars are some examples, but you may find others that are a mix of these or are unique. The point is to find your identity, your voice.

Be Persistent and Consistent

Once you've figured out who your audience is, what they worry about, and what your identity is, the last step is to be persistent and consistent in your messaging. When you pitch to reporters, bring all these elements together to tell a story.

Remember, telling a story is *not* selling them on how great your company is! That's called self-promotion, and that will fail if that's all you do.

For example, if your software helps secure health-care organizations, the story is that data breaches of patient data can be hugely damaging for companies. Give the reporter some newsworthy statistics on what types of health-care organizations get breached, how often it happens, etc.

Tell the reporter three points to your story such as:

- Cybersecurity personnel are harder to find due to a shortage.
- Because of advances in technology such as big data and machine learning, software can help automate some of the tasks you once had to hire for.
- Results have seen accuracy shoot up from 30 percent to 90 percent.

Next you blend your avatar in. Your company wasn't involved in health care but because of the overwhelming demand for its software (reluctant hero), it's now installed in multiple hospitals across the nation.

Play off any of the three points in your story in different ways, and use it consistently in all your media outreach or press releases. Be persistent but not a pest! That's a fine line to walk. Following these four steps will have you on the road to successful PR.

How PR Is Like Sales

There's an old saying that the only function that matters in a company is marketing. After all, without a market or customers, there are no sales and ergo no company.

Another truism that is just as appropriate in public relations should be that all PR is simply sales. Think about this for a moment. In sales you are approaching prospective clients and customers with the ultimate intent of selling products or services.

In sales you need to create a prospect list. The quality of the list can play a big part in your success in terms of how close they match your offerings. In sales you approach the prospects, pitch them, and try to close them. In sales, especially these days and in higher-end goods, *building personal relationships is crucial.*

Similarly, in PR you are approaching prospects (editors or reporters) with the ultimate intent of selling them your story idea.

In PR you also need to create a targeted list of media. Simply blasting your release to the world, or worse yet, spamming media that aren't in the area of interest, is at best a waste of money and a good way to get yourself blacklisted by said media.

> ### RepGold Tip:
> Building long-term relationships with the media can be very helpful. You want to position yourself not just as a self-promoter, but more importantly a source of valuable information when they are on deadline. If you help them, I guarantee you it can only pay dividends in the future.

In PR you conduct outreach to the media, whether via cold emails, phone calls, social media channels, or live in person. It will take multiple attempts to get an editor or reporter to respond. The sad truth is the vast majority of reporters will never respond. It's simply because they are too bombarded with dozens of pitches every day.

In PR the pitch is all-important. What is your story idea? Why would their readers care? Why is it relevant? What facts do you have to back it up? How unique is it? Is there a tie-in to any major story currently in the news? In PR you need to close the deal, meaning get a commitment from the media so that they will run a story that includes you.

So reexamine your public relations efforts with a critical sales eye. It can reap massive benefits in the form of more media coverage for you.

HOW TO BE A REPORTER'S BEST FRIEND

Good PR is just like good sales. In other words, building relationships works in sales. Building and nurturing relationships is also essential to long-term success in PR. My image of a reporter brings to mind the character of Lois Lane or Clark Kent: always in a hurry, banging away at the typewriter, and constantly looking for a scoop or breaking story.

As print media continues the transition to online, reporters are under even more pressure to deliver more stories with fewer resources. Online also means 24 hours a day, 365 days per year, so they are constantly looking for stories because they are delivering and updating news around the clock. Any newsworthy content that you can help them with is a very good strategy.

Here are some ways to be a reporter's best friend:

1. Avoid sending emails with attached documents. This is a common rookie mistake. It means more likely than not, your email will be snagged by their spam or antivirus filter and not make it to their inbox. Or if it does make it to their inbox, the reporter may not open it for fear of a virus. Instead, cut and paste the words from any document directly into the body of the email. This goes for press releases especially.

2. If they are on deadline and need something, get it to them. Reporters are almost always on deadline. This means that they have a hard deadline to get all materials in for publication. If you are contributing to a reporter's story who is on deadline, you better make sure you can deliver what you promised to them in time. If you don't, your future requests may go straight to the trash bin.

3. Be honest. Nothing gets you blacklisted by the press faster than lying. This could be in the form of the actual facts or data you're pitching. It could be in promising an exclusive but instead allowing competing outlets to run with a story. It could be making promises of getting them info for their deadline. Honesty is always the best policy.

4. Like any good salesperson, put yourself in the reporter's shoes. What do they want to hear from you? What story ideas would fit their specialty? What are their pain points and how can you help them with that? The best reality check is the "so what" question. If you were the reporter and you read what

was being pitched to you, would you say, "So what?" In other words, is there an actual story here?

5. Help make their job easier. You will get brownie points by helping reporters even if it doesn't directly benefit you in this particular story. Again, since they are always on deadline, they greatly appreciate it if you can help them find or verify statistics, facts, or quotes. Make sure formatting is all simple and correct, with your grammar and spelling checked and double-checked. Doing this greatly increases the chance that you will be successfully "source filed" with the reporter, meaning they will note that you are a knowledgeable and reliable source for future stories. It's a good way to get your company or executives mentioned here and there.

6. Don't sell to them, sell for them. Another common mistake is selling your company or product to the reporter. Here's the honest truth: The reporter and their readers don't really care about you. What they do care about are interesting stories that impact them. One simple trick is to research stories that are already being covered in the media and find a way to link your story to these popular ones. For example, any trends in products such as the iPhone, politics, environmental news, pop culture, etc.

ARE PRESS RELEASES EXTINCT?

In the early 2000s when the internet, search engines, and the phrase "search engine optimization" were just gaining popularity, press releases were underrated. With the newer wire services providing distribution at prices everyone could afford, including MarketWire (now Marketwired), PRWeb, and PR.com, businesses of all sizes started using press releases to "do PR."

As press releases began to be used and abused by everyone, the public relations industry claimed that the press release was effectively dead as a tool. The truth, as always, is somewhere in between.

If you expect that writing and distributing a press release will lead to reporters calling you for media coverage, you will be in for disappointment. The average reporter gets bombarded with hundreds of press releases and pitches each and every day. From a sheer numbers perspective, the odds that your press release will be the one that catches his or her eye is slim.

But that doesn't mean there aren't uses for the press release. Here are some of the advantages of regular writing and distribution of press releases:

1. **Makes news public.** Even if reporters don't pick up the story and run it as exclusive, certain news sites such as Yahoo! or MarketWatch will run the press release verbatim (depending on the wire service, which all have different distribution agreements with different news sites). This makes the news you are announcing officially on the public record, for all to see.

2. **Builds a time line of credibility.** The biggest hurdle most businesses have to overcome is to convince their website visitor that their company is legitimate and trustworthy. This is especially true for B2B firms as well as small-to-midsize companies. Having a press section with a regular history of press releases every month or two can reassure prospects or clients that your business is active and engaged and not a fly-by-night operation. The flip side is that press releases need to be done on a consistent basis to avoid large gaps of time when there are no press releases at all. It may lead visitors to wonder why nothing was happening for such a long period of time.

3. **Helps with search engine optimization (SEO).** As press releases get picked up on blogs or news sites, the wise use of including targeted keywords can help your SEO efforts through: a.) creating inbound links to a website, even if they

are "no follow," which is better than no links, and b.) creating news stories so that when someone searches your company's name, they see that you are active. You could potentially have the press release coverage itself rank high on search engines for certain keyword phrases.

4. **Builds a foundation for PR.** Press releases are still the backbone of many PR campaigns when you approach the media. Here are some ideas for press releases. It would be a good idea to map out the next six months and allocate what potential story ideas would fit at what month.
   a. New products
   b. New customers/wins
   c. Partnerships
   d. Acquisitions
   e. New hires/promotions/org changes
   f. Events and shows
   g. Speaking/public appearances

Check out the appendix at the end of this book for 104 ideas for press releases.

RepGold Tip:

Remember, just a press release itself is not enough for effective PR. Success in PR requires a mind-set of sales. You need to be constantly building relations and working story angles with the press. But done right, a press release can be a valuable part of that process.

What's the Deal with Wire Services?

There's a lot of misconception about what wire services are, how they work, and what they can do for you. In this section I want to give readers a clear idea of the real benefits and limitations of wire services, which can end up costing a lot more money. I've set this up as a Q and A, sort of like an FAQ feature.

Q: What is a wire service?
A: You may have heard the term "news just crossing the wires" on TV or the radio. From a public relations standpoint, companies can put out press releases on something called a wire service. The wire service then distributes the press release to the world and it officially is "live." Some notable wire service companies include PR Newswire, BusinessWire, Marketwired, and PRWeb. There are quite a few others out there, but for the most part these four offer a good cross section.

Q: What's the difference between the wire service companies?
A: This is the $64,000 question. You would think the more expensive the wire service, the more effective it is. Unfortunately, the answer isn't that simple. The short answer is, it depends. It depends on a.) your budget and b.) your goals.

If you have a fairly large PR budget, going with a bigger wire service such as PR Newswire or BusinessWire can be beneficial. *But* that doesn't mean the lower-cost wire services have nothing to offer. While it is true that more of the top journalists subscribe to PR Newswire or BusinessWire, that may mean very little in the end, because …

Q: How effective are wire services?
A: … it is debatable just how effective a wire service is in getting you press. A common rookie mistake is to think that PR is just writing a press release and slapping it on the wire service, then sitting back

and waiting for the phone to ring from breathless reporters. Unfortunately, the reality is completely different.

RepGold Tip:

The average journalist today is slammed with information. Hundreds of pitches emailed daily. Constant wire service distributions of press releases. Phones ringing with PR people on the other end. Tweets and Facebook posts. The fact is, if you're solely relying on a wire service to get you media coverage, you'll be severely disappointed.

Pros of Using Wire Services

- Officially makes an announcement or news "live" or public
- Keeps your customers, partners, stakeholders, investors updated on your company
- Builds a public record of consistent news and progress
- Some sites will pick up releases off the wires and run them almost word for word, also known as syndication
- Wire service pages rank relatively high on Google, which is useful for online reputation management purposes

Cons of Using Wire Services

- Because wire services were overused by SEO professionals, Google has come to devalue their pages over time. This means they may not rank as high as they used to.
- The high-end services can be *very* expensive, easily $1,000 per release or more
- Doesn't help you get actual unique, dedicated press coverage with target reporters

- Lulls you into a false sense of progress for your PR initiatives

Overview of Wire Services

Like any recommendation, be sure to verify our information first, as things change rapidly.

EXPENSIVE: PR NEWSWIRE

Widely considered the granddaddy of wire services, PR Newswire is also the most expensive. Most journalists pay attention to PR Newswire if it's related to their beat. National distribution in the United States plus a photo or two can easily run you over $1,000 per release. Reporting features are quite robust. Recommended for larger companies or publicly traded companies. Smaller companies may want to consider putting out very important announcements on PR Newswire, such as funding announcements, new product launches, key customer wins, major awards won. Wire services usually have a word limit (sometimes around 800) with additional charges for each set of words after that (usually by the next 100 words or so).

EXPENSIVE: BUSINESSWIRE

BusinessWire is about as well respected as PR Newswire while slightly less expensive. Like PR Newswire, they charge for photo distribution and have different rates for different types of distributions (geography, industry, media). National distribution can run you maybe 25 percent less than PR Newswire. Recommended for mid- to large-size companies or publicly traded companies.

MODERATE: MARKETWIRED

Marketwired hits the sweet spot of distribution breadth while not being quite so expensive. Rates are about 50 percent less than the top two. Marketwired is a good choice for companies seeking wider distribution but without the budget for the top two.

INEXPENSIVE: PRWEB

There are many other cheap or free wire services around, but PRWeb is now part of Vocus, a large media company, and thus likely more reputable and reliable. The cheapest package starts from a low $99 flat, with tiered upgrades up to over $300. Unlike the others, their fee isn't based on word count. They also allow you to post two photos free of charge. Reporting leaves something to be desired; the web clips simply direct you to Google News. Distribution is also not as wide as the other, more expensive services. Recommended for start-ups, entrepreneurs, and announcements that aren't that "important" (such as new executive hires, exhibiting at a trade show, small promotions, etc.).

RepGold Tip:
There's a company called eReleases that is a wholesaler of PR Newswire. You can distribute via eReleases for only $399 and get about the same benefits than if you bought the $1,000+ package directly from PR Newswire. Your press release will look as if it were sent out from PR Newswire.

The Dirty Secret of Wire Services

One account executive from a wire service firm that I won't name told me that the dirty secret most don't know is that the level of distribution within the United States doesn't really make a difference in terms of pickup. In other words, whether you spend $1,200 on national distribution or $400 on just the state of California, the pickup will actually be about the same. From my experience this seems to be the case, but your mileage may vary. Your best bet if you use one of the top two services is to use a state distribution and pick a few micro-lists that are highly targeted to your industry.

Remember …

Wire services are a means to an end, *not* an end in itself. They are simply tools to help you achieve your PR goals. They shouldn't be confused as PR in its entirety. Nothing substitutes the ability to reach out personally to highly targeted press contacts with compelling story ideas. But they certainly have a role to play in immunizing your brand for ORM purposes. Just be sure to use wire services judiciously.

Why and How to Include Links in Press Releases

Most marketers understand how press releases fit into the scheme of public relations. It's a very useful tool in that regard. What they may not be aware of is that a press release can kill two birds with one stone. Done properly, you can use a press release to help build natural links to your website that would help your ranking on Google.

In marketing speak, this is called "link building for SEO." The term "link building" may stir up some negative images in your head. But when you get down to it, link building is simply getting legitimate links from other websites to yours. That's it. And the more "relevant" links to your website, the more Google (and other search engines) like it.

Note that links you get via press releases are almost always "no follow," which is a technical term that means Google doesn't value them highly. There's a debate within the industry of the value of "do follow" versus "no follow" links. But the consensus seems to be that having some "no follow" links is better than having no links at all.

Here are how press releases can help you build those links:

1. Press releases put out on a wire service are picked up by many, many websites. They are often syndicated and run word for word automatically. For instance, press releases sent out over PR Newswire will be sometimes reprinted on Yahoo! or MarketWatch. Some of these sites are directly relevant to your industry and subject matter. So again, relevance.

2. By their nature, press releases are written about particular

topics. So the words surrounding the links add context. Relevance again!

3. As I mentioned earlier, some news sites will run your press release word for word. Others will rewrite them, edit them, shorten them; they are creating different variations of the content for the links on your behalf!

4. Google News links are always useful for SEO purposes. Think about it. Any story on Google News must have been pre-vetted, so it instantly has trust in the eyes of Google. Check out https://news.google.com/ if you don't believe me.

Here's how to include links in your next press release:

First, always include your company's URL in the "boilerplate" of your press release. The boilerplate is the "About Us" section near the bottom. For instance, here is Firecracker PR's boilerplate:

> About Firecracker PR
> Firecracker PR is a boutique agency that helps companies get known, period. Our proven 5-step "Ignites" process helps scale awareness quickly. We blend the best of traditional and digital public relations and marketing. Learn more about us at http://www.firecrackerpr.com.

Second, try as much as possible to use "http://" for links. Without it, many links won't be clickable.

Third, you can turn any snippet of text into a clickable link. Instead of saying "Go to http://www.firecrackerpr.com to learn more about technology PR," you can say "Click here to learn more about technology PR" and make this entire sentence a link. In SEO lingo, that is the anchor text of the link. All you do is highlight the text you want to turn into a link, go to Insert, then select Hyperlink. Enter the URL, and voilà, it's a link! These instructions are for Microsoft Word, so check with your own word-processing software for how to insert a hyperlink.

Fourth, make sure the wire service you use allows you to have these clickable links in the text of your press release. Not all of them do, certainly not the free ones. Most limit the number of clickable links for obvious reasons.

CAUTION:

Overuse of this type of anchor text for link building may lead to a Google penalty. When in doubt, stick with the URL itself, or hyperlink a segment of a sentence rather than keyword phrases. Avoid constantly using the same anchor text with the same key-words. That used to work a long time ago. Today, it's a good way to raise red flags with Google.

The Art of the Exclusive

While the goal of public relations is always to get press coverage for your company, products, or executives, there's always been this mystique about the "exclusive." Truth be told, most stories simply aren't interesting enough to be considered for an exclusive.

While everything about your business to you might seem worthy of being on the cover of the *Wall Street Journal*, the truth as you can guess is far harsher.

Remember, the first rule of PR is that you need to put yourself in the shoes of the reporter or editor. Is your breaking story really interesting enough that an editor would consider it for an exclusive? Be brutally honest with yourself.

The job of any PR firm worth their salt is to help come up with news stories that would indeed be considered newsworthy. But when a story does get exclusive coverage in a major outlet, watch out. That grand slam could generate a lot of positive coverage. An exclusive story can be syndicated by other major news outlets. It can also open doors for future stories.

The funny and interesting thing about PR is that press begets press. That is, if you get press, it's easier to get more press. But isn't that a conundrum? How do you get press in the first place if that's the case?

And that is the hardest part about any new business. Cracking that first barrier to get press coverage.

In one example, our public relations agency Firecracker PR was able to land one of our clients an exclusive story on TechCrunch. The beauty of this is that, besides the high number of readers that TechCrunch has, many other sites also just pull stories off TechCrunch for their own use. The end result was massive downloads for their new iPhone app within the first week, wildly successful beyond our initial plans. It was so successful that it crashed their servers.

In another example, our agency helped an artificial intelligence client land an exclusive in the *Wall Street Journal*. We researched and narrowed it down to three reporters that would be interested in the story. Then we tailored the pitch to the "beats" (or areas) that the reporter writes about. For instance, the reporter that eventually wrote the story covers the Venture Capital (investment) world. Since the story was about a Series B investment round closing, it was a natural fit for him.

The downside of an exclusive may be that other outlets don't want to write about the news once one outlet has covered it. But it still can be a great option for getting some top-tier media coverage.

How can your business benefit from a potential exclusive? Here are a few steps:

1. **Make sure you indeed have something newsworthy.**
   As I said, just because you think it's interesting doesn't mean

the editor will. Is it really groundbreaking? Is it first in its field? What about this makes it so unique that a reporter just has to write about it now? Is it timing around a holiday or event?

2. **Get familiar with the target outlets and reporters.**

Read the stories to get a feel for their coverage area. Note their tone of voice, how technical they are, etc. Pitching an exclusive is like pitching a normal story, only far harder. Therefore, to maximize your odds, you must familiarize yourself with the reporter you're going to pitch. Visit their Twitter account or LinkedIn page and make sure they are covering the "beat" (or area) that your business is involved in.

3. **Start building a media contact list.**

Research all the contact information you can about the target reporters: their email, LinkedIn profile, social media accounts. Many news sites will have them under About Us or Contact Us, or often in another subpage called Editorial Contacts or Masthead. If they don't and just have a generic email address or form, it's time to do some research. Google their name + "email" and see what comes up. Look for them on LinkedIn. If you don't, upgrade to the paid Premium account on LinkedIn. This will enable you to send what's called "InMail" to people. You can then send them the pitch through LinkedIn. Or find out what their Twitter handle is, and directly tweet them. Or try Facebook or Google +. Essentially in this day and age it should be possible to find some way to contact any journalist.

4. **Sharpen your pitch.**

Your pitch will make or break your chances. Pay particular attention to the subject line, which accounts for the vast majority of opens. Try using their first name in the subject line, like: "Courtney, an exclusive story pitch on new social media app." Another popular approach is to use "Appropriate person" in the subject line. Or write a subject line like you would a headline if you were the reporter. Something intriguing enough that they just have to read further. From there, make a comment about something that you found in your research. It could be about an article they wrote or where they live or their background. It shows them you took the time to research and you're not just cutting and pasting a generic email. Tell them why this story would be of interest to their readers. Why should they care? Then "always be closing" (ABC). Ask if they'd like the story as an exclusive, and if so, to let you know by such and such a date. Promise that you will not release the story for two days after they run it. This gives them the reassurance that they will be putting something out that no one else will have, a rarity in this day and age of saturated media.

5. **Work your way down.**
Start your pitch for the exclusive story from the outlet you most want coverage in. From there, work your way down to the smaller or less desired outlets. Follow up a couple of times and give them a few days each to respond.

6. **Don't make promises you can't keep.**
This is a good rule of thumb for PR in general. If you break your promise to a journalist, kiss any future story goodbye. If you promise only they will get the story, then keep your promise.

7. **Ride the wave.**
Once the exclusive story hits and the promised time has elapsed, you can ride that wave of coverage to get additional coverage. Other journalists note what is being covered, and they won't want to be left out of a big story either. So getting an exclusive should help you get more coverage in the future.

8. **Promote it!**
Post it on your social media accounts, post it to your News section of the website, forward it to your sales team for use, join and post it to relevant LinkedIn groups, post it to an appropriate sub-Reddit. With just a little planning and work,

you can turn a story idea into a lot of press coverage by mastering the art of the exclusive!

Should You Outsource PR or Hire Internally?

Should you outsource to a public relations agency or hire someone as a permanent employee? Both have their pros and cons, but keep in mind the actual cost of hiring someone as an employee is more than just their salary. In fact, the total all-in cost to bring someone into the company could be over 50 percent more than just the salary. Check out appendix B for a breakdown of additional costs that must be factored in when hiring employees.

Of course, there are pros and cons with both approaches.

With an employee, one benefit is that if they are on a salaried basis, you can usually give them more work to do than an agency who is billing you on an hourly rate or monthly retainer. Employees tend to be more focused and dedicated to the company. Because they are living and breathing your business, they will come to know your product intimately.

The downside is it can be hard to find a suitable employee in your immediate area that matches both the qualifications and salary you want to pay. Employees can also bring headaches, especially if they turn out to be problematic. Firing an employee requires more careful consideration and may have legal repercussions.

Agencies bring a team of experienced PR pros to the table, saving you the time of hiring individuals. They generally have a set process in place on how to onboard new clients and quickly work to start creating awareness through fast media coverage. You'll also be benefiting from the collective wisdom of many people versus just one employee.

The downside of agencies is that they may not be able to provide as many hours as a full-time salaried employee can bring. There's also less oversight of an agency versus a worker who is in your office. Then there's the question of focus. Agencies tend to manage multiple accounts. Will they give you the same dedication that you deserve?

There's no easy answer, but carefully weighing the pros and cons can help you come to an arrangement that fits your particular needs the best.

Here are some general guidelines of when you should consider hiring an employee:

- If you have a set hierarchy of internal marketing people—including a VP of Marketing, a Director of Marketing, and so on—who can assist the new internal PR person to integrate into the company's marketing team
- If your company's PR needs are relatively straightforward, such as simple press releases, some minor media outreach, assisting with events, preparing for reviews …
- … or conversely your PR needs are exceptionally complex and industry-specific, for instance a niche type of health-care field
- If your PR needs require exceptional hours, for instance attending many trade shows in person
- If your company has the bandwidth to hire and onboard an internal employee
- If you believe the extra cost of an employee is a long-term wise investment

Here are some general guidelines for when you might want to consider hiring a public relations agency:

- If your PR needs are for the short term, consider hiring an agency for a 90- or 120-day project
- If you don't want to deal with the headaches of hiring and managing an employee
- If your internal marketing team is small and overworked
- If you prefer the flexibility and ease of being able to let an agency go
- If your PR needs are more complex, finding an agency with

the expertise in your industry might be the best course of action. For instance, our agency Firecracker PR specializes in helping technology companies. Often their content can be complex and require in-depth understanding to properly execute a communications strategy. Compare that to, say, a maker of smartphone cases whose PR needs are going to be much simpler.

Of course, arrangements may vary depending on your specific needs. Many companies, and indeed some of our clients, have an in-house PR resource while also using an agency. These tend to be larger companies with bigger marketing budgets to tap into.

Small businesses might think they are priced out of the game. But many agencies specialize in helping small businesses who are on limited budgets. You might even want to consider hiring a contractor to do one-off work from websites such as Upwork or PeoplePerHour.

When No Amount of PR Can Save You

As a partner in a public relations and marketing agency, I like to think that both can have a huge positive impact on the outcome of a business. The truth of the matter is, sometimes the fundamentals of a business are in such poor shape and the trajectory is going in such a terminal way that no amount of PR campaigns can halt the slide. In this way, it's critical to realize the role of PR and marketing. They help spread the word on what you're really good at.

But they can seldom staunch the decline of a company that has more-fundamental flaws. One of the most famous examples of this is RIM's Blackberry. Once a legend of a device that was used by all corporate power players, then presidents, then consumers, today the Blackberry is just another obsolete artifact in the history of tech. Yet at its peak, Blackberry was on top of the world with no threat in sight.

Actually, there was a threat in sight. And therein lies the problem. Apple was hard at work on their new iPhone that was set to revolutionize the mobile-phone industry. And Google was preparing their Android phones to counter Apple. What did RIM do? Initially they stuck their head in the sand and believed that with their superior keyboard, loyal corporate users would never defect.

Let's call that a slight underestimation to be kind.

In fact, the "cool" factor of an iPhone, combined with all sorts of new abilities to watch videos, listen to music, surf the web, and play games, pretty much trumped the better keyboard of the Blackberry. And corporate users basically ignored IT departments and brought their own devices to use, to the point now where most companies have given up and implemented actual BYOD (Bring Your Own Device) policies.

By the time RIM finally acknowledged the threat, they tried all sorts of shifts in business strategy … all to no avail.

Today, RIM is a cautionary tale—another casualty of the ever-changing technology industry. With such an onslaught, no amount of positive spin on the situation could help. In fact, the co-CEOs were ridiculed for being oblivious to the situation they were in, and being overly optimistic when the writing on the wall was clear to even the most casual observer.

This situation is by no means unique. In fact, technology has vastly accelerated the time to obsolescence for products and services.

Once-famous brand names like Compaq, MySpace, Blockbuster, and Blackberry found out the hard way how disruptive technology could be. The top book in this area is *The Innovator's Dilemma* by Clayton M. Christensen (Harvard Business Review Press, 2016). Its premise is that leaders in an industry are caught between a rock and a hard place. The very thing that brought them success is also the thing that prevents their ability to innovate.

Moral of the story? Take a hard, honest look at your business and the competitive horizon. If you aren't willing or able to innovate, even in the face of clear competitive threats, no amount of public relations or marketing will save you.

In fact, a PR agency may be able to provide you with valuable guidance in a similar way that top consulting firms are hired to do. Because PR agencies are active in the market, and because they aren't biased as internal company employees might be, they may be able to see the forest in spite of the trees. With their pulse firmly on what direction the market is headed, they can provide valuable insight for your executive team in terms of company strategy, new product development, and positioning.

The One Key to Successful Content Marketing

Most content marketing efforts fail, and it usually isn't pretty.

Companies can spend tons of budget and time on creating beautiful content. They toil for months, then post it on Facebook … and wait.

Nothing happens.

You can't be faulted if at this point you think "content marketing is a waste of time." It is if that's how you do it. Here's the one key to success in content marketing:

Know who you're going to promote the content to before *you create the content.*

Too often, companies create content for the sake of creating it. Is it any wonder that a "fire, aim, ready" strategy isn't working?

Here's a case study on how we took a lowly infographic and ended up with:

- A dedicated article in Mashable (PR)
- An extremely valuable back-link from Mashable (SEO)
- Over 1,300 social shares (viral and social media)
- A top ranking on Google (SEO)

Is your infographic getting those results? Our client was a software company for human resources. Sounds boring, right? The point of this case study is that any "boring" topic can be parlayed into massive marketing results with the right foresight and planning.

1. **Find a Hot Topic—"Newsjacking"**
   At that time, one of the top stories in the news was that Yahoo! had just hired a new CEO, Marissa Mayer. When she came in, one of the first things she did was change the HR policy: no longer were employees allowed to work remotely. This caused quite an uproar. Almost every news site was talking about it, debating its pros and cons.
   Using our Step 4 in Firecracker's "Ignites" strategy— "Newsjacking"—we took advantage of a trending topic.
   Newsjacking is finding a hot news item and finding a way to leverage it. In our case, we wanted to create an infographic around the subject.

2. **Research Who Reports on This News**
   Prior to doing a single thing in creating the infographic, we put our PR hats on and did some research. Using a combination of media databases, social media, and Google, we identified a list of reporters and bloggers who wrote about telecommuting. We made a list and found their email addresses and social media handles.

3. **Determine the Probability for Success**
   Based on the list we had created and the articles they had written, we then assessed our chances for success. PR and content marketing aren't guaranteed successful results. But you can "stack the deck" so you maximize your odds for success.
   That's just what we did. We found a hot news topic. We identified the reporters who write on the topic. Based on this, we determined our chances were good. All systems were go.

4. **Create the Infographic.**
   Believe it or not, this was the easy part. As I've mentioned

previously, only 20 percent of your effort should be on content creation. Eighty percent of your effort should be on researching and promoting the content.

Using publicly available statistics, we put together a Word document of brainstorming items. From there, we grouped them into similar themes. Then we took a red pen and edited it down to something manageable. The actual graphic design of the infographic was done by an outsourced designer. We gave him creative direction and themes, and he put together a pretty decent infographic.

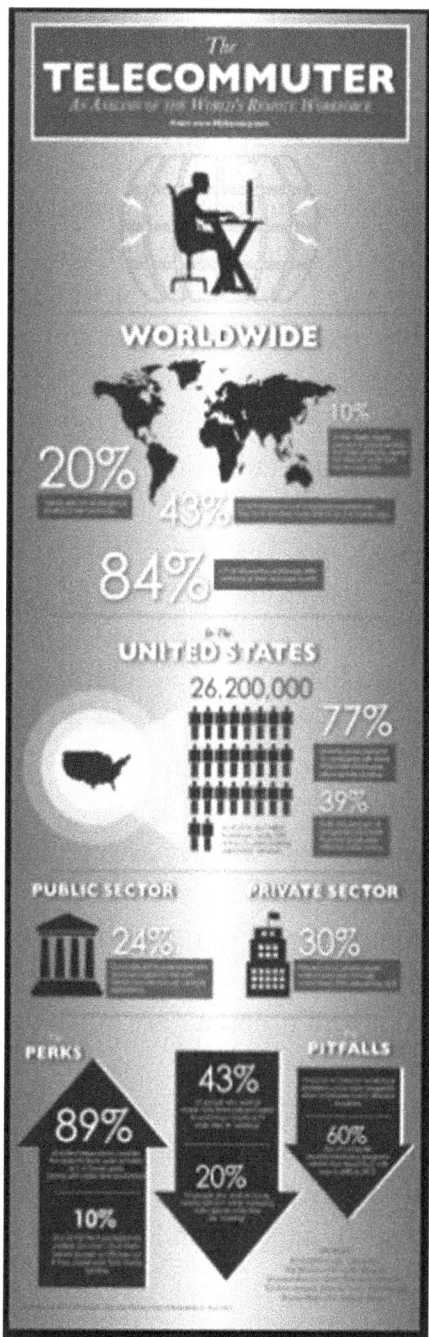

Remember: a relevant topic and statistics will trump a pretty-looking infographic any day.

1. Promote, Promote, Promote

   The infographic was done. It was placed on our client's website, with social-sharing buttons up and SEO tags (title and description) created. Now came the fun part of PR outreach. We personally emailed each reporter and blogger one by one. No mass email blasts using programs such as Constant Contact. Through persistent emails and follow-ups, we got a nice long Mashable article out of it.

2. Measure Results

   The results were awesome from that one article alone:

   - Because Mashable has such high trust and authority in the eyes of Google, that article itself ended up ranking no. 2 overall on Google for the search term "telecommuter infographic."
   - The reporter of the article gave credit to my client and a nice juicy link to my client's web page where we had put up the infographic. For those who know anything about SEO, high-quality back-links are one of the top factors for success. And it doesn't get much better than a Mashable link.
   The Mashable article itself had over 1,300 social shares!
   - Because of that link, my client's web page where the infographic lived ranked no. 1 for "telecommuter infographic," even higher than Mashable.

Also because of that link, the infographic was the first result on Google Images as well.

Now that's what I call a successful content marketing campaign.

So next time before you even start creating content, remember the key to success:

RepGold Tip:
Know who you're going to promote the content to before you spend even one second on design.

PR and SEO Strategy: Using Awards

The different fields of marketing are converging. Once separate silos are now intertwined. A good example of this is public relations and search engine optimization (SEO).

Done right, good PR can lead to real benefits to SEO. Here's a tactic on how a simple PR campaign can lead to massive SEO gains.

Brian Dean's blog, Backlinko, is a must-read for anyone serious about SEO. Having purchased his Advanced Link Building Course, I found it to be well worth the price.

One of the strategies he espoused involved creating an award, notifying the winning websites, and reaping the benefits of those who end up linking to you.

For example, if you create an award of the Top 100 Websites in some field, and 10 percent link to you, that's ten quality back-links.

Beyond just the SEO back-link benefit, there's a definite PR benefit here as well. Creating an award gives you instant credibility in the eyes of your reader, especially if it's well thought out with a nice award logo. You can also use it to reach out to bloggers in that field and see if they won't link to it.

The Award Strategy is an example of how the lines between PR and SEO continue to blur. This can be a definite advantage to those who know how to leverage the ins and outs of each to gain the benefits.

Here's the simple (but time-consuming) steps we took to get results. First, we spent time up front researching all dog websites we could find. We then curated the best and sorted them in alphabetical order using a spreadsheet.

Second, we created an award for these top dog websites. Using contractors we created a nice professional award logo and a page where they could download the logos for winners.

Third is the fun part. We simply contacted the owners of the website to inform them that they had won! And who doesn't like to win awards? We told them where to download the logo and gave them the link to the client's website where all the top dog websites were.

Out of the ninety-five websites listed on our award page, about ten actually responded and linked in some way to our site. This was either done through the logo that had a hyperlink, in a mention on their blog, or on other parts of their website.

What does that mean for PR? You get exposure to the built-in audiences of those ten websites.

What does that mean for SEO? You get ten high-quality, relevant, natural do-follow back-links to your site.

Are you beginning to see the possibilities? This should get you excited!

Again, you can tell this is on the labor-intensive side of things as it requires research and writing descriptions. Then it involves a lot of manual outreach and follow-up. But the potential benefits can be enormous.

If you spent the time to properly research good websites, then the website owners who are listed will be more than happy to show off their new award. People researching on the internet may come across this list looking for top dog websites and spend a lot of time reading the content (high "Time on Site" makes you look good in the eyes of Google).

As I said, bloggers on dogs or pets may link to this if it's well done. It's truly a win-win-win. What's the takeaway from this? As the fields of PR and other areas of marketing change and the lines between them blur, keep looking for innovative ways to get results.

9

CONCLUSION

Hopefully by the time you've reached this section, you'll have realized that success in the field of online reputation management is an ever-moving target.

The fact that most of the tactics I've discussed were discovered through trial and error should give you hope that there are likely new tactics still to be discovered. And as Google's algorithm continues to change (or perhaps the search engine landscape changes one day and a new competitor displaces Google), ORM will in fact necessitate being flexible.

The core philosophy to follow is to carry out activities that would genuinely impact the reputation of a product, service, company, or individual in positive ways. If you do that, then no matter how much search engine algorithms change, you maximize your chances of protecting your online reputation.

I also want to repeat something I've said elsewhere in this book, which is that ORM as a discipline is really a merger of other disciplines such as SEO, public relations, social media, and customer service.

The formula I came out with:

$$ORM = SEO + PR + SM + CS^2$$

… likely will need to be updated as the world of marketing changes.

My desire was to give you actionable advice that could help you immediately, while providing inspiration for new ideas that you might come up with that aren't listed here.

Once you have that mind-set, you will be able to invent new ways to impact ORM that large agencies or companies haven't even thought of. The power of the internet is such that knowledge is power, and any individual or small business with that knowledge can have a disproportionate impact.

Should you ever need to outsource your public relations, search engine marketing, social media, or entire ORM function, look up our agency at www.FirecrackerPR.com.

APPENDIX A: 104 IDEAS FOR PRESS RELEASES

Press releases remain a great tool to get media coverage and build your company's credibility.

Public relations is often referred to as "earned media," because boy, do you earn it.

Unlike advertising where you buy your awareness, getting written about by the press comes down to a combination of timely story ideas, creativity, tenacity, and some good ol' fashion luck.

Caveat: I want to make it clear that simply writing a press release and putting it on the wire service will *not* lead to you being on the front page of a leading news website. As I've said, a press release is a tool. And like any tool, it is only as useful as its handler. And also like any tool, it depends on how well the tool is crafted.

Caveat #2: If you're struggling to think of what to write about for a press release, it might mean that you have nothing really newsworthy at the moment.

Meaning if you try to force it, the reporters you pitch to will see right through the junk.

Just because we're presenting 104 ideas doesn't mean you issue crummy press releases for the sake of it.

Don't ever put out a press release unless it is truly newsworthy.

So with that out of the way, let's keep going.

The following guide can help you plan your PR calendar ahead of time, so you won't have to scramble and decide what to write and when to publish it.

Although this list is pretty exhaustive, it's not exclusive by any means.

SEASONAL TOPICS

1. Back-to-school promotion
2. Christmas
3. Thanksgiving
4. Black Friday
5. New Year's
6. Valentine's Day
7. Easter
8. Spring break
9. Graduation
10. Mother's Day
11. Father's Day
12. July 4
13. Summer break
14. Labor Day
15. Halloween
16. Tax day
17. Presidential election

New!
18. Brand-new product release
19. Updated new version of product

20. New website
21. New blog
22. New blog post
23. New trademark
24. New patent issuance
25. New uses for product/service

Promotions
26. Discounts
27. Product bundles
28. Free giveaways
29. Handouts
30. Social media contest
31. Contest
32. Live events
33. Celebrity tie-in
34. Sporting event
35. Trade show display
36. Speaking at live event
37. Award nomination
38. Award grand prize winner

Company Information
39. Grand opening
40. Expansion
41. New major client
42. New facilities/moving
43. New executive hire
44. Certification
45. Membership in an association
46. Company anniversary
47. Response to complaint/controversy
48. Response to lawsuit

49. Filing of a lawsuit
50. Customer number milestone
51. Case studies
52. Customer service initiative
53. Recognition of partner achievements
54. Partner program announcements
55. New distributor

Company Employees
56. Awards won by specific employees
57. New training programs for employees
58. Qualifications by employees
59. Retirement of key employee
60. Appointment/promotions into new positions
61. Committees
62. Email to employees

Nonprofit
63. Charity partnership
64. Charity event
65. Charity donation per sale
66. Company contribution to community
67. Employees volunteering to charity
68. Sponsoring local programs or events
69. Scholarships
70. Pro-bono work

Community
71. Open days or community exhibits
72. Organize a tour
73. Honor an institution
74. Host a debate
75. Issue a protest

76. Issue a commendation
77. Disaster response
78. Green initiative

Media

79. Book
80. Upcoming radio interview
81. Upcoming TV interview
82. Media appearance
83. New online videos
84. New course

Information & Content

85. Industry research/market share
86. Prediction/projections/forecasts on industry trend
87. Publication of new content
88. Infographic
89. Survey
90. Report
91. Studies
92. Podcasts
93. Contrarian view
94. Expert view on issue

Piggyback on Hot Issues

95. Piggybacking on current political events
96. Piggybacking on current entertainment news
97. Piggybacking on current pop-culture memes
98. Piggybacking on current health trends/scares
99. Piggybacking on current business issues
100. Piggybacking on current technology

Financial Results
101. Quarterly earnings results
102. Investors conference call
103. Investors meeting/conference
104. Annual sales information

APPENDIX B:
TOTAL COSTS TO
HIRE AN EMPLOYEE

This is a hypothetical example of bringing a junior-level public relations specialist on as an employee. The more experienced the hire, the more the salary will be.

Costs	Estimated (example)	
Salary and benefits		
Proposed salary	$50,000.00	
Benefits		
Medical	$10,000.00	
Dental	$2,000.00	
Vision	$1,000.00	
401 K	$5,000.00	
Subtotal	$68,000.00	

Administrative Costs	Hours	
Calculating benefits and salary (cost/hour)	2	$100.00
Working with IT to develop workspace	0.5	$42.50
Contracting with re-cruiter/headhunter		$5,000.00
Advertising for position		$300.00
Screening résumés	4	$200.00
Interviewing candidates		
First interview	2	$250.00
Second interview	1	$125.00
Final interview	1	$125.00
Mileage and entertainment		$100.00
Credit/background/refer-ence check		$150.00
Test for controlled sub-stances		$75.00
Relocation/moving costs		$2,000.00
Subtotal		$8,467.50
Orientation/training		
In-house training on com-pany applications	6	$210.00
Training programs with vendor		$600.00

Administrative Costs	Hours	
Additional office equipment		$500.00
Tech support	2	$70.00
Subtotal		$1,380.00
Total hiring costs		$77,847.50

INDEX

ABOUT THE AUTHOR

Edward M. Yang is founder and Managing Partner for Firecracker PR, an award-winning public relations and marketing agency based in Orange County, California. With over two decades of experience advising companies ranging from Fortune 500 brands to tech startups, Yang has been published in outlets such as Entrepreneur.com. Yang was born in Pullman, Washington, and spent time living in Vancouver, Canada, as well as Taipei, Taiwan. He earned his Bachelor of Arts degree from the University of British Columbia, and his MBA from the Paul Merage School of Business at the University of California Irvine.

www.ingramcontent.com/pod-product-compliance
Lightning Source LLC
Chambersburg PA
CBHW050526190326
41458CB00045B/6727/J